Crochet
Scarves
Fabulous Fashions –
Various Techniques

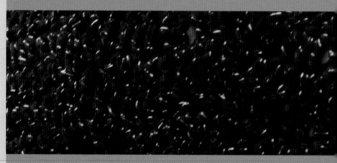

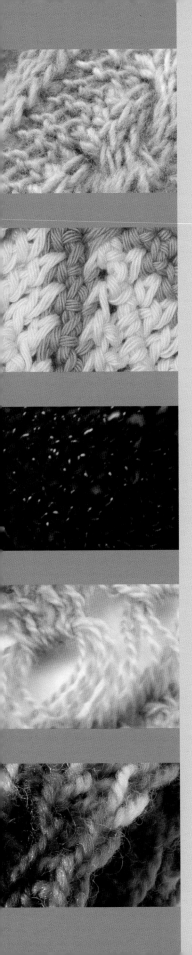

Crochet Scarves

Fabulous Fashions – Various Techniques

Sharon Hernes Silverman

Photographs by Alan Wycheck

STACKPOLE
BOOKS

Published by
STACKPOLE BOOKS
5067 Ritter Road
Mechanicsburg, PA 17055
www.stackpolebooks.com

Printed in U.S.A.

10 9 8 7 6 5 4 3 2 1

First edition

All designs © Sharon Hernes Silverman, www.SharonSilverman.com
Photographs by Alan Wycheck
Cover design by Caroline Stover
Standard yarn weight system chart and skill level symbols used courtesy of the Craft Yarn Council of America (CYCA), www.craftyarncouncil.com/standards.html.

Library of Congress Cataloging-in-Publication Data

Silverman, Sharon Hernes.
    Crochet scarves : fabulous fashions in various techniques / Sharon Hernes
  Silverman ; photographs by Alan Wycheck. — First Edition.
      p.   cm.
  Includes index.
  ISBN 978-0-8117-0081-8
    1. Crocheting—Patterns. 2. Scarves. I. Title.
TT825.S5442 2012
746.43'4—dc23
                                           2012005461

Contents

Acknowledgments

Many thanks to everyone who helped this book take shape.

I am grateful to those who provided supplies: Stella Balian of Abuelita Yarns; Barbara Lundy Stone and Demian Savits of Blue Heron Yarns; Peggy Wells of Brown Sheep Company, Inc.; Lijuan ("Jojo") Jing of Jojoland; Gail Callahan of Kangaroo Dyer; India Donaldson and Patty Lyons of Lion Brand Yarn Company; David Van Stralen of Louet North America; JoAnne Turcotte of Plymouth Yarn Company, Inc.; Stephanie Alford of SpaceCadet Creations.

Finished project photos were shot in the beautiful galleries and courtyard at the Art Association of Harrisburg, as well as along the riverfront across the street. Thanks to association president Carrie Wissler-Thomas and her staff for their gracious hospitality. I encourage everyone to visit this gem in Pennsylvania's capital city.

Thank you as always to photographer Alan Wycheck for his collaboration and indispensible visual contributions to this, our fifth book together.

I am grateful to Mark Allison, editor, and Judith M. Schnell, publisher and vice president of Stackpole Books. Kathryn Fulton, Sarah Wolf, Caroline Stover, and other members of the Stackpole Books team also brought their editorial, design, marketing, and publishing expertise to this project.

Thanks to the Craft Yarn Council of America for permission to reprint charts, to the Crochet Guild of America (CGOA) for industry information and news, and to The National NeedleArts Association (TNNA) for its support of yarn industry professionals.

My interaction with other designers and crafters—in person and electronically—has been extremely valuable. Special thanks to the Ravelry correspondents who have been my cheerleaders, sounding boards, information sources, and all-around helpful colleagues.

I could not have completed this project without the support of my friends and family, especially my husband, Alan, and our sons, Jason and Steven.

How to Use This Book

This book is for people who are already comfortable with basic crochet stitches (chain, single crochet, double crochet). Before you start the projects, review the basic instructions in the back of the book if needed.

Seven of the patterns are done in Tunisian crochet. If you have not used this technique before, I hope you will give it a try! Tunisian crochet allows you to use your crochet hook to create fabrics that look knitted or woven. All of the basics are explained in the back of the book.

Whenever I use a special stitch or technique, the instructions are included with the pattern. Step-by-step photographs appear throughout, to supplement the detailed instructions. In addition, symbol charts are provided. These focus on specific parts of the patterns that benefit from visual representation and are included to help make the patterns easy to understand. Instructions on how to read charts are in the Techniques section.

Reference material, including supplier information for yarn and hooks, appears at the end of the book. There is also a visual index in which you can see all of the projects at a glance.

Scarves

Accordion Arrows

SKILL LEVEL

■■■□
INTERMEDIATE

This yarn caught my attention with its festive colors and interesting construction. Each ball is actually a solid color yarn wrapped with threads in different hues.

The pattern plays off the theme of a mitered square. You can use as few or as many colors as you like—I chose six, but Tequila comes in thirteen punchy shades if you want to try more.

MEASUREMENTS

50 inches (127 centimeters) by 4.5 inches (11.4 centimeters)

MATERIALS

ONline Linie 258 Tequila, 44% cotton, 44% acrylic 12% viscose, 1.76 ounces/50 grams, 88 yards/ 80 meters

4

Medium

Color A: Baby Green Rainbow Multi (09), 1 skein

Color B: Bubble Gum Rainbow Multi (04), 1 skein

Color C: Yellow Rainbow Multi (07), 1 skein

Color D: Aqua Rainbow Multi (06), 1 skein

Color E: Lilac Rainbow Multi (02), 1 skein

Color F: Coral Rainbow Multi (11), 1 skein

Crochet hook size K (6.5 mm) or size needed to obtain gauge

Crochet hook size J (6.0 mm), or one size smaller than primary hook, for edging

Stitch marker

Tapestry needle

STITCHES AND ABBREVIATIONS

Chain stitch (ch)

Fasten off (fo)

Loop (lp), loops (lps)

Right side (RS)

Single crochet (sc)

Single crochet 2 together (sc2tog)

Slip stitch (sl st)

Stitch (st), stitches (sts)

Wrong side (WS)

Yarn over (yo)

GAUGE

Gauge is flexible for this project. Suggested gauge for a single mitered square is 4.5 inches (11.4 centimeters) across widest point, unblocked.

For gauge swatch, work in pattern from beginning to end of first segment. If your gauge is accurate, use your gauge swatch as the first square in the pattern.

Special Stitch

Single Crochet Two Together (sc2tog)

This makes a single crochet decrease by turning two stitches into one. In this pattern, it is used on the edging where two colors meet.

Insert hook in next st, yo, pull up lp (2 lps on hook).

Insert hook in next st, yo and pull up lp (3 lps on hook).

Yo, pull through all 3 lps.

Scarf

First Segment

Foundation: With A, ch 2. Work 3 sc in second ch from hook. Place stitch marker to mark as RS.

Row 1: Ch 1, turn. Sc in first st, 3 sc in next sc, sc in last st.

> **NOTE** Each row is worked with a sc in each st up to the middle, 3 sc in the middle st, then 1 sc in each remaining st.

Row 2: Ch 1, turn. Sc in each of next 2 sc, 3 sc in next sc, sc in each of next 2 sc.

Row 3: Ch 1, turn. Sc in each of next 3 sc, 3 sc in next sc, sc in each of next 3 sc.

Row 4: Ch 1, turn. Sc in each of next 4 sc, 3 sc in next sc, sc in each of next 4 sc.

Rows 5–10: Continue in this fashion. Each row adds 2 sc. In Row 10, there are 10 sc on each side and 3 at the point (total 23 sc). Fo.

Following Segments

Row 1: With RS facing, place first segment so the starting point is at the bottom and it is a diamond shape. Join B in the seventh sc on the top of the right-hand side, counting from the point on the right-hand side.

Ch 1 (counts as sc). Sc in each of the next 4 sc, 3 sc in next sc, sc in each of the next 5 sc.

Row 2: Ch 1, turn. Sc in each of next 6 sc, 3 sc in next sc, sc in each of the next 6 sc (on this row only, the final sc is in the top of the initial ch from the previous row).

Rows 3–6: Continue in this fashion, adding 1 sc on each side until there are 10 sts on each side and 3 at the point (total 23 sc). Fo.

Add segments in colors C, D, E, and F, then in colors A through F twice. Total 18 segments.

Edging

With RS facing, use smaller hook to attach any color other than A or F in the right-hand point of the final segment.

Ch 1. Sc in each st up to apex, 3 sc in next st, sc down left side to left point. Work 2 sc in st at point, sc evenly down side of block to last st in that color. Sc2tog in final st of current block and first st in next block.

Continue down left side, working 2 sc on points and sc2tog in final st of one color and first st of next color.

At bottom point of scarf, work 3 sc. Sc evenly up right-hand side, again working 2 sc at each point and sc2tog at each color change. Join to first st with sl st. Fo.

Finishing

Using tapestry needle, weave in ends. Lightly steam block on WS if desired.

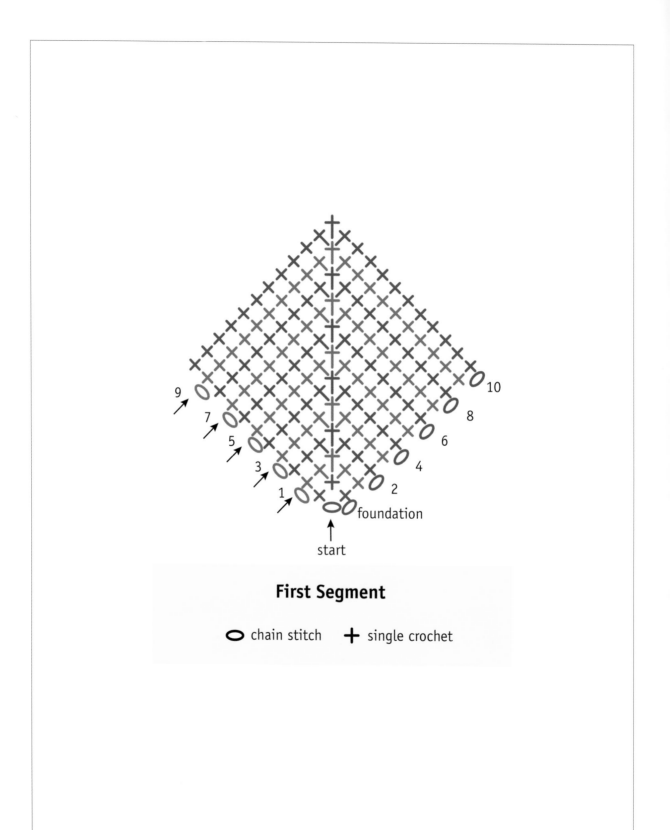

First Segment

○ chain stitch   ✛ single crochet

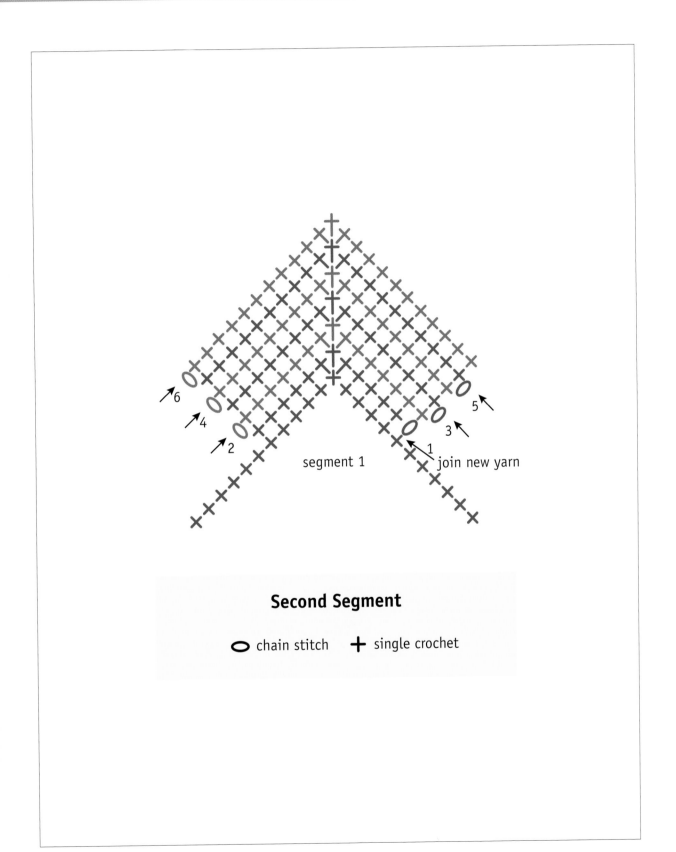

segment 1

join new yarn

Second Segment

⬭ chain stitch   ✚ single crochet

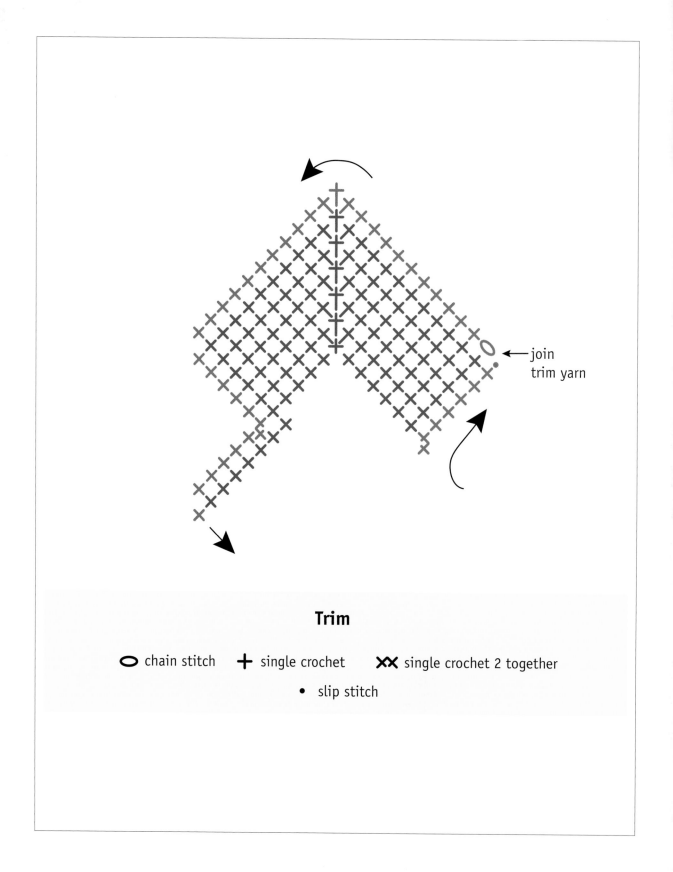

join
trim yarn

Trim

○ chain stitch   ✛ single crochet   ✗✗ single crochet 2 together

• slip stitch

Berry Sorbet

SKILL LEVEL

INTERMEDIATE

Blue Heron's Egyptian Mercerized Cotton in the Blueberry colorway looks lovely in long stitches like double trebles and in dense arrangements like bobbles. This scarf gives you a bit of both. Delicious!

MEASUREMENTS

57 inches (144.78 centimeters) by 4 inches (10.2 centimeters)

MATERIALS

Blue Heron Egyptian Mercerized Cotton, 100% cotton, 8 ounces/227 grams, 1,000 yards/ 914 meters

Super Fine

Blueberry: 1 skein (project uses approximately 375 yards/343 meters)

Crochet hook size H (5.0 mm) or size needed to obtain gauge

Tapestry needle

STITCHES AND ABBREVIATIONS

Chain space (ch-sp)

Chain stitch (ch)

Double treble crochet (dtr)

Fasten off (fo)

Large Bobble (LB), Large Bobbles (LBs)

Loop (lp), loops (lps)

Right side (RS)

Single crochet (sc)

Skip (sk)

Slip stitch (sl st)

Stitch (st), stitches (sts)

Wrong side (WS)

Yarn over (yo)

GAUGE

22 stitches and 15 rows in sc/4 inches (10.2 centimeters) blocked

For gauge swatch, ch 26.

Row 1: Sc in second ch from hook and in each ch across. Total 25 sc.

Row 2: Ch 1, turn. Sc in each ch across. Total 25 sc.

Repeat Row 2 until swatch measures 4.5 inches (11.4 centimeters).

Special Stitches

Large Bobble (LB)

The large bobble joins 5 dc stitches together at the top and the bottom.

[Yo, insert hook as instructed, yo, pull up lp, yo, pull through 2 lps] in same spot 5 times. Total 6 lps on hook. Yo, pull through all 6 lps, ch 1.

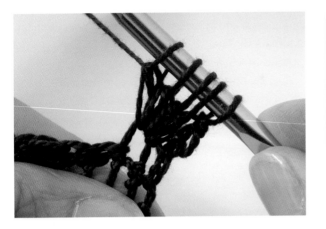

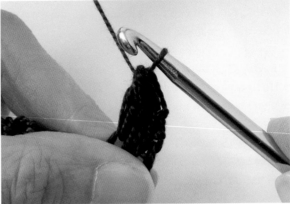

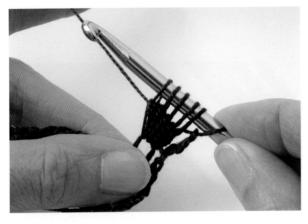

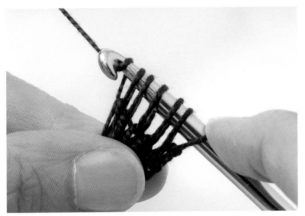

Double Treble Crochet (dtr)

Wrap yarn around hook 3 times. Insert hook as instructed. Yo, pull up lp (5 lps on hook). [Yo, pull through 2 lps] 4 times.

Scarf

Chain 19.

Row 1 (RS): Sc in second ch from hook and in each ch across. Total 18 sc.

Row 2: Ch 1, turn. Sc in each sc across. Total 18 sc.

Rows 3–5: Repeat Row 2.

Row 6: Ch 3, turn. Sk first sc. *LB in next sc, ch 1, sk 1 sc. Repeat from * across, ending with LB in last sc. (Bobbles poke out on the right side.) Total 9 LBs.

NOTE There are 2 chs in a row at the end of each bobble, one that closes the bobble and one that skips over the single crochet below.

Row 7: Ch 3, turn. Sk LB, work LB in next ch-sp. *Ch 1, sk LB, LB in next ch-sp. Repeat from * across, working last LB under turning ch from previous row (not into a ch). Total 9 LBs.

Rows 8–15: Repeat Row 7.

Row 16: Ch 1, turn. * Sc in top of LB, sc in ch-sp. Repeat from * across, working last sc under turning ch. Total 18 sc.

Rows 17–21: Ch 1, turn. Sc in each sc across. Total 18 sc.

Row 22: Ch 5 (counts as dtr), turn. Sk sc at base of chs. Dtr in next sc and in each sc across. Total 18 dtr.

Row 23: Ch 5 (counts as dtr), turn. Sk st at base of chs. Dtr in next st and in each st across, ending with dtr in top of turning ch. Total 18 dtr.

Rows 24–25: Repeat Row 23.

Row 26: Ch 1, turn. Sc in top of each dtr across, working final sc into top of turning ch. Total 18 sc.

Rows 27–31: Ch 1, turn. Sc in each sc across. Total 18 sc.

Repeat Rows 6–31 three times. Repeat Rows 6–21. Fo.

Finishing

With tapestry needle, weave in ends. Lightly steam block scarf on WS.

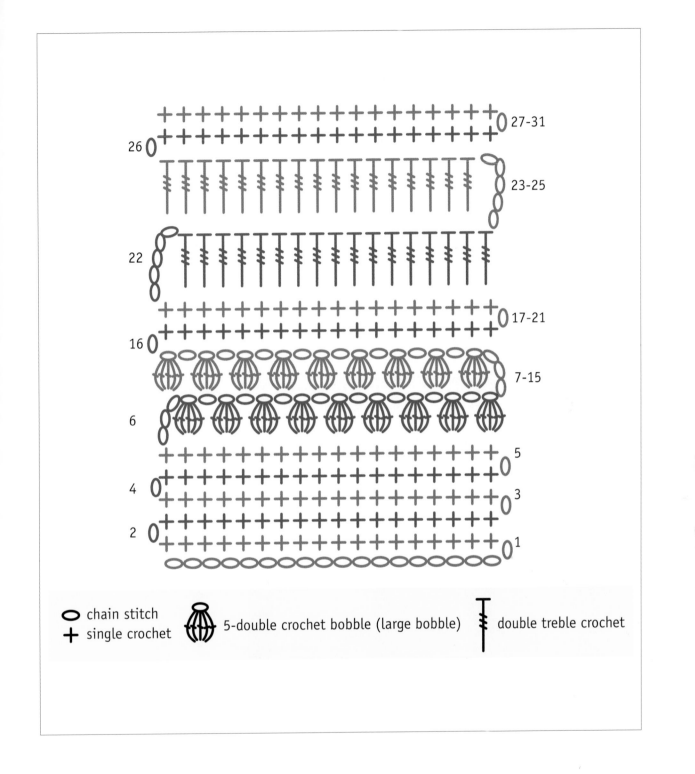

Sparkly Scarlet

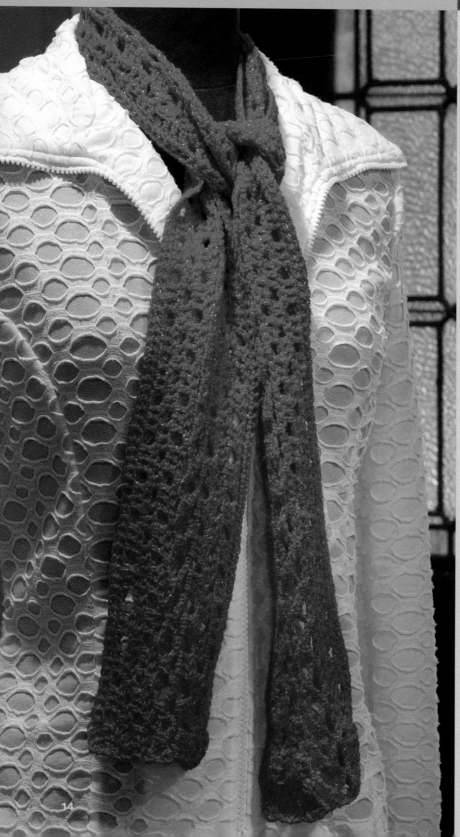

SKILL LEVEL

■■□□

EASY

Bright red yarn with metallic accents is used for this festive scarf, which is quick to crochet in an openwork pattern. If you need to whip up a last-minute gift (or an enhancement to your own wardrobe), this is your go-to pattern.

MEASUREMENTS

57 inches (144.8 centimeters) by 3.75 inches (9.5
centimeters)

MATERIALS

Vanna's Glamour, 96% acrylic, 4% metallic polyester,
1.75 ounces/50 grams, 202 yards/185 meters

2

Fine

Ruby Red (113), 1 skein

Crochet hook size I (5.5 mm) or size needed to obtain
gauge

Tapestry needle

STITCHES AND ABBREVIATIONS

Chain (ch), chains (chs)

Chain space (ch-sp)

Double crochet (dc)

Fasten off (fo)

Right side (RS)

Single crochet (sc)

Skip (sk)

GAUGE

Gauge is flexible for this project. Suggested gauge
is 18 stitches and 8 rows in dc/4 inches (10.2
centimeters), unblocked.

For gauge swatch, ch 25. Last 3 chs count as first dc
of Row 1.

Row 1: Dc in fourth ch from hook and in each ch
across. Total 23 dc.

Row 2: Ch 3 (counts as dc), turn. Sk st at base of chs.
Dc in each dc across, ending with dc in top of
turning ch. Total 23 dc.

Repeat Row 2 until swatch measures at least 4.5
inches (11.4 centimeters).

Scarf

Ch 218.

Row 1 (RS): Sc in second ch from hook and in each ch
across. Total 217 sc.

Row 2: Ch 3 (counts as dc), turn. Sk the sc at base of chs.
*Dc in each of next 3 chs, ch 1, sk 1 sc. Repeat from * un-
til 4 sc remain. Dc in each of remaining 4 sc.

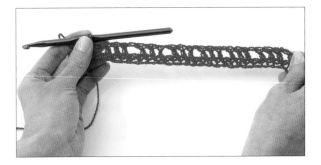

Row 3: Ch 3 (counts as dc), turn. Sk st at base of chs.
Dc in next dc, ch 1, sk 1 dc. *Dc in next dc, dc in ch-sp, dc
in next dc, ch 1, sk 1 dc. Repeat from * across, ending with
with 1 dc in last dc and in top of turning ch.

Row 4: Ch 3 (counts as dc), turn. Sk st at base of chs.
*Dc in next dc, dc in ch-sp, dc in next dc, ch 1, sk 1 dc. Re-
peat from * across until 4 sts remain. Dc in next dc, dc in
ch-sp, dc in next dc, dc in top of turning ch.

Row 5: Ch 1, turn. Sc in first dc. *Ch 5, sk 3 dc, sc in next ch-sp. Repeat from * across until 4 dc remain. Ch 5, sk 3 dc, sc in top of turning ch.

Row 6: Ch 5, turn. Sc in ch-5 sp. *Ch 5, sc in next ch-5 sp. Repeat from * across. Ch 2, dc in last sc.

Row 7: Ch 1, turn. Sc in dc. Ch 3 (sk ch-2 sp and sc), sc in ch-5 sp. *Ch 3, sc in next ch-5 sp. Repeat from * across.

Row 8: Ch 3 (counts as dc), turn. Work 3 dc into ch-3 sp. *Ch 1, sk sc, work 3 dc into next ch-3 sp. Repeat from * to last ch-3 sp. Ch 1, work 3 dc into ch-3 sp, dc into sc.

Row 9: Repeat Row 3.

Row 10: Repeat Row 4.

Row 11. Ch 1, turn. Sc in each dc and ch-sp across. Total 217 sc.

Finishing

Using tapestry needle, weave in ends.

Do not steam or iron this scarf. It holds its shape very well and should not require blocking. If you do want to block it, wet it with cool water, gently squeeze it dry, then pin it into shape with non-rusting pins on a blocking board or thick towel. Allow to air-dry completely.

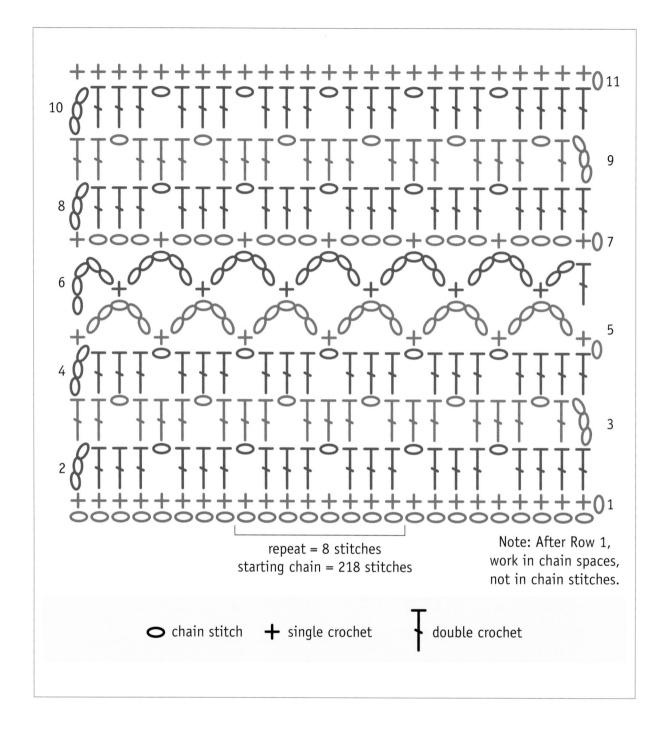

repeat = 8 stitches
starting chain = 218 stitches

Note: After Row 1,
work in chain spaces,
not in chain stitches.

⚬ chain stitch   + single crochet   ⊤ double crochet

Crisp Green Apple

SKILL LEVEL

■■□□

EASY

The frosted stitch in Tunisian crochet is one of my favorites. I used it here to make a chic, skinny scarf. Sirdar Snuggly Baby Bamboo yarn has excellent stitch definition and a lovely sheen.

MEASUREMENTS

53 inches (134.6 centimeters) by 2.5 inches (6.4 centimeters), plus 5 inches (12.7 centimeters) of fringe at each end.

MATERIALS

Sirdar Snuggly Baby Bamboo, 80% bamboo, 20% wool, 1.76 ounces/50 grams, 104 yards/ 95 meters

Light

Color A: Apple Green (155), 1 ball

Color B: Pearl White (131), 1 ball

Color C: Taupe Grey (140), 1 ball

Tunisian crochet hook size F (3.75 mm) or size needed to obtain gauge

Tapestry needle

6-inch (15.2 centimeter) piece of cardboard for making fringe

STITCHES AND ABBREVIATIONS

Chain (ch), chains (chs)

Fasten off (fo)

Loop (lp), loops (lps)

Right side (RS)

Skip (sk)

Slip stitch (sl st)

Tunisian simple stitch (Tss)

Wrong side (WS)

Yarn over (yo)

GAUGE

Gauge is flexible for this project. Suggested gauge is 22 stitches and 17 rows in Tss/4 inches (10.2 centimeters), blocked.

For gauge swatch, ch 25. Work 20 rows in Tss.

Scarf

With A, ch 15.

Row 1 forward (RS): Insert hook in second ch from hook, yo, pull up lp. *Insert hook in next ch, yo, pull up lp. Repeat from * across. Total 15 lps on hook. Do not turn.

Row 1 return: Yo, pull through 1 lp. [Yo, pull through 2 lps] twice. *Ch 1, yo, pull through 4 lps, ch 1. [Yo, pull through 2 lps] three times. Repeat from * until 1 lp remains on hook.

> **NOTE** This differs from a standard Tunisian crochet return. Pulling through 4 lps where indicated creates the pointed clusters that are the hallmark of this stitch pattern.
>
> All returns are worked this way.

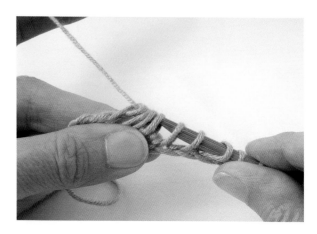

Row 2: Sk first vertical bar. Tss in each of next 2 sts. *Insert hook under next ch, yo, pull up lp; insert hook into lp of center of cluster on previous row, yo, pull up lp; insert hook under next ch, yo, pull up lp. Tss into each of next 3 sts. Repeat from * across, working final Tss into the vertical bar and the horizontal thread behind it for stability. Return as for Row 1.

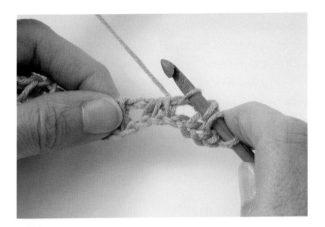

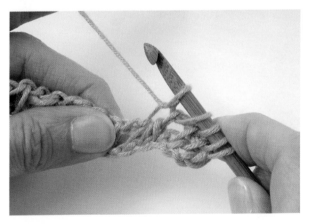

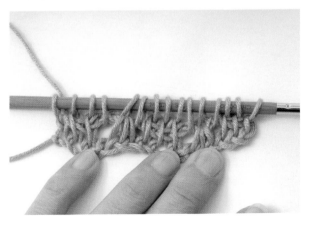

Rows 3–20: Repeat Row 2, changing to B when 2 lps remain on the return pass of Row 20.

> **NOTE** After changing color, cut old color, leaving approximately a 4-inch tail.

Rows 21–40: Repeat Row 2, changing to C when 2 lps remain on the return pass of Row 40.

Rows 41–60: Repeat Row 2, changing to A when 2 lps remain on the return pass of Row 60.

Rows 61–239: [Work 20 rows in A, 20 rows in B, 20 rows in C] twice, then 20 rows in A, 20 rows in B, 19 rows in C.

Row 240: Sk first vertical bar. [Insert hook in next vertical bar as for Tss, yo, pull up lp, yo, pull through both lps (sc made)] twice. Insert hook under ch, yo, pull up lp, yo, pull through both lps. Insert hook in the top of the cluster, yo, pull up lp, yo, pull through both lps. Insert hook under ch, yo, pull up lp, yo, pull through both lps.

Continue in sc across, inserting hook as for pattern sts. Fo.

Finishing

Using tapestry needle, weave in ends. Lightly steam block scarf on WS if desired.

Fringe

There are seven sets of fringe on each end. Each set consists of one strand folded over to make two strands.

Loosely wrap A around cardboard 5 times, wrap B around cardboard 5 times, wrap C around cardboard 4 times. Cut bottom edge of yarn to make 14 strands.

NOTE I arranged the colors randomly. Use a different arrangement or make your fringe all one color if you prefer.

Take one strand of yarn and fold it in half. With RS of scarf facing you, slip crochet hook from back to front of scarf through one stitch. Pull folded end of fringe through from front to back. Slip both cut ends through the folded part of the fringe. Pull taut. Attach fringe evenly across the bottom and across the top of the scarf. Make one knot in each strand of fringe, in a random pattern.

Lightly steam block fringe. Trim fringe so it is even, at approximately 5 inches (12.7 centimeters) long.

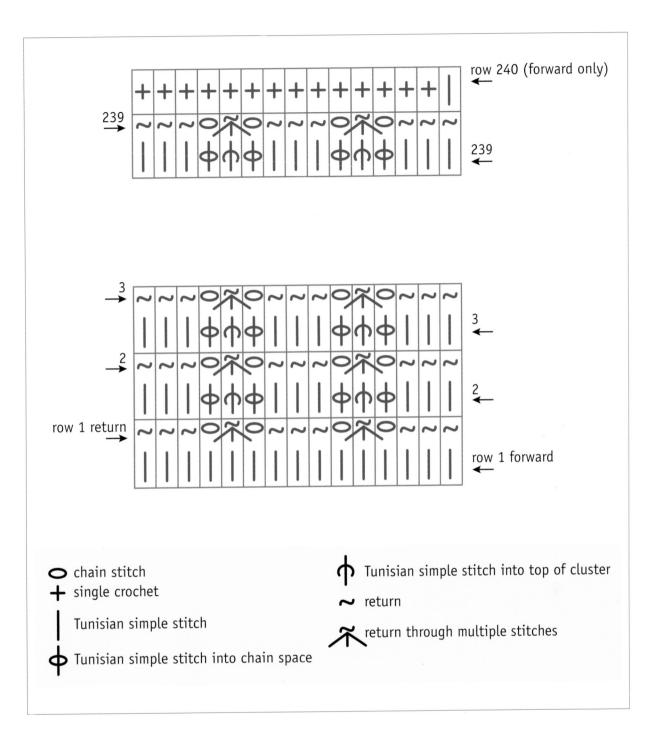

row 240 (forward only)

239

239

3

3

2

2

row 1 return

row 1 forward

O chain stitch
+ single crochet

| Tunisian simple stitch

Φ Tunisian simple stitch into chain space

φ Tunisian simple stitch into top of cluster

~ return

return through multiple stitches

Marabou

Projects made with woven yarn always make people gasp, "How did you do that?!"

Truth be told, the yarn does most of the work. Open up the textured strand and work near the top edge—ignoring the rest—and you'll see cascades of ruffles start to appear. The key is to use a hook that's large enough to make big stitches but small enough to get through the netting without tearing it.

The stitches in this project are basic; it is rated as "Intermediate" difficulty because it takes some practice to get used to the yarn. With a little time and patience, you'll soon be flaunting an astonishing scarf of your own.

MEASUREMENTS

48 inches (122 centimeters) by approximately 5 inches (12.7 centimeters) when ruffles are fluffed out. The core of single crochet stitches measures 2 inches (5 centimeters) wide.

MATERIALS

Katia Tul, 82% combed cotton, 18% polyamide (nylon), 1.76 ounces/50 grams, 27 yards/25 meters

Medium

Ecru (56), 2 skeins

Crochet hook size K (6.5 mm) or size needed to obtain gauge

Sewing needle

Sewing thread, ecru

STITCHES AND ABBREVIATIONS

Chain (ch), chains (chs)

Fasten off (fo)

Loop (lp), loops (lps)

Single crochet (sc)

Yarn over (yo)

GAUGE

NOTE Since the core of the scarf is so narrow, gauge is measured over 2 inches (5.1 centimeters) for stitches, and over 4 inches (10.2 centimeters) for rows.

Gauge is flexible for this project. Suggested gauge is 8 stitches/2 inches (5.1 centimeters), 6 rows/ 4 inches (10.2 centimeters) in sc, measuring core stitches only, not ruffles.

For gauge swatch, ch 9.

Row 1: Sc in second ch from hook and in each ch across. Total 8 sc.

Row 2: Ch 1, turn, making sure you can see the stitches you will work into. (If you've turned the wrong way, those stitches will be obscured by the yarn.) Sc in each sc across. Total 8 sc.

Rows 3–6: Repeat Row 2.

NOTE If your gauge is accurate, you can use your gauge swatch as the beginning of the actual project.

Special Stitches

Ch and Sc with Woven Yarn

NOTES Instead of a traditional "yarn over," you'll be inserting the hook about a quarter inch below the top of the netting—straight through the fabric—to serve that function.

When you turn at the end of a row, go clockwise (for right-handers) so you can see the stitches you'll work into on the next row. If you turn the wrong way, the stitches will be obscured by the yarn. Because you will always turn the same direction, you may have to stop and untwist the yarn once in a while.

To ch: Stretch the top edge of the yarn out to reveal the netting. Insert hook through the netting about a quarter inch from the top, a few inches in from the end. (You'll sew the ends in later.)

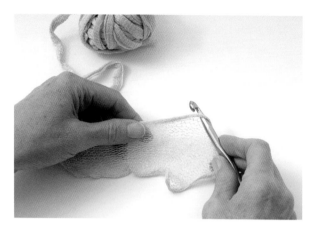

Insert the hook into the netting about an inch away. This counts as a yo. Pull through lp (ch made). Continue in this fashion, unfurling the yarn as you go.

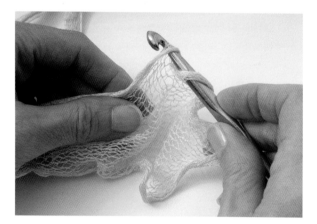

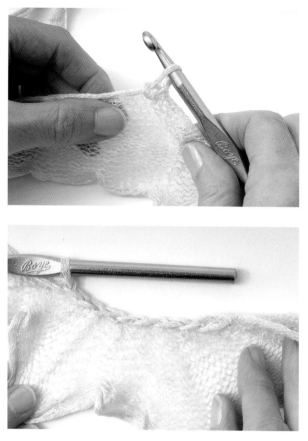

To sc: Insert hook into ch (or sc) as indicated. Make sure you are going through the space made by the st, not through the netting.

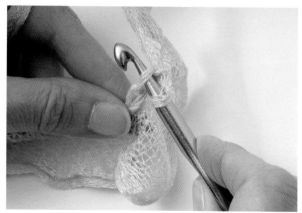

Insert hook into unworked yarn about an inch away. This counts as a yo. Pull up a lp (2 lps on hook). Insert hook in yarn about an inch away. Again, this counts as a yo. Pull through both lps. Sc made.

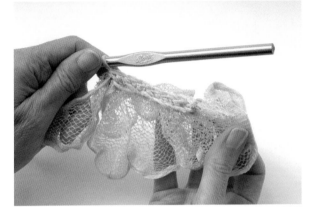

Scarf

Ch 9. (You'll sew the ragged end in later.)

Row 1: Sc in second ch from hook and in each ch across. Total 8 sc.

Row 2: Ch 1, turn, keeping ruffle to back. Sc in each sc. Total 8 sc.

Repeat Row 2 until scarf measures 48 inches (122 centimeters) long.

Fo.

> **NOTE** When you run out of yarn and have to start a second skein, leave approximately 3 inches of the old yarn and the new yarn loose. You will sew these ragged ends in later.

Finishing

Fold in ends from the first row, final row, and where you ended one skein and started the next. Don't fold so tightly that the yarn makes a hard ridge, just tightly enough to hide the ragged edges. Sew those ends in place with sewing needle and matching thread.

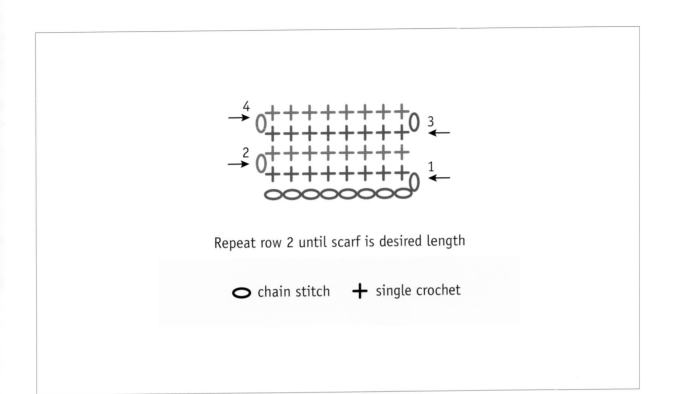

Repeat row 2 until scarf is desired length

O chain stitch **+** single crochet

Changing Tides

SKILL LEVEL

■■■■

EXPERIENCED

This stitch pattern, with its floating blocks of single crochet worked sideways within a row, has intrigued me for a long time. My experiments revealed that it looks best with a solid-color yarn, one that is soft enough to be comfortable yet structured enough to do justice to the pattern. Plymouth Jeannee, a cotton/acrylic blend, fills the bill.

The color changes from blue to sand, like water on a beach. Is the tide coming in, or is it receding? That depends on your perspective.

MEASUREMENTS

68 inches (172 centimeters) by 7 inches (17.8 centimeters)

MATERIALS

Plymouth Jeannee DK, 51% cotton, 49% acrylic, 1.76 ounces/50 grams, 136 yards/124 meters

3

Light

Color A, medium blue (10): 2 skeins

Color B, ecru (07): 2 skeins

Crochet hook size G (4.25 mm) or size needed to obtain gauge

Tapestry needle

STITCHES AND ABBREVIATIONS

Chain (ch), chains (chs)

Chain space (ch-sp)

Double crochet (dc)

Fasten off (fo)

Loop (lp), loops (lps)

Right side (RS)

Single crochet (sc)

Skip (sk)

Stitch (st), stitches (sts)

Wrong side (WS)

GAUGE

14 stitches and 7 rows in dc/4 inches (10.2 centimeters), blocked

For gauge swatch, ch 23. Last 3 chs count as first dc on next row.

Row 1: Dc in fourth ch from hook and in each ch across. Total 21 dc.

Row 2: Ch 3 (counts as dc), turn. Sk st at base of chs. Dc in each dc across, ending with dc in top of turning ch. Total 21 dc.

Rows 3–9: Repeat Row 2.

Scarf

Foundation: With A, ch 38.

Row 1 (RS): Sc in second ch from hook and in each ch across. Total 37 sc.

Row 2 (WS): Ch 1, turn. Sc at base of ch and in each sc across. Total 37 sc.

Row 3: Ch 3 (counts as dc), turn. Work 2 dc into st at base of those chs. *Ch 3, sk 5 sts, sc in next st, ch 3, sk 5 sts, [3 dc, ch 1, 3 dc] into next st. Repeat from * once. Ch 3, sk 5 sts, sc in next st, ch 3, sk 5 sts, 3 dc into final st.

Row 4: Ch 3 (counts as dc), turn. Work 2 dc into st at base of those chs. *Ch 3, sc in next sc, ch 3, [3 dc, ch 1, 3 dc] into ch-sp in center of dc fan. Repeat from * once. Ch 3, sc in next sc, ch 3, 3 dc into top of turning chs.

Row 5: Ch 3 (counts as dc), turn. Work 2 dc into st at base of those chs. *Ch 6, sc in second ch from hook and in next 4 chs (total 5 sc). [Ch 1, turn, sc in each sc across floating block (total 5 sc)] twice, anchor floating block to previous row with a sc in next sc, turn, sc in each sc across floating block (total 5 sc), turn, [3 dc, ch 1, 3 dc] into ch-sp in center of dc fan. Repeat from * once. Ch 6, sc in second ch from hook and in next 4 chs (total 5 sc). [Ch 1, turn, sc in each sc across floating block (total 5 sc)] twice, anchor floating block to previous row with a sc in next sc, turn, sc in each sc across floating block (total 5 sc), turn, work 3 dc into top of turning ch.

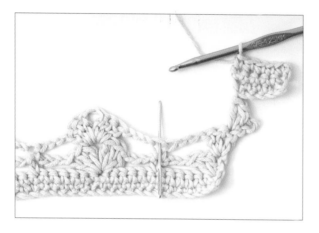

Row 6: Ch 3 (counts as dc), turn. Work 2 dc into st at base of those chs. *Ch 3, sc into top corner of floating block, ch 3, [3 dc, ch 1, 3 dc] into ch-sp in center of dc fan. Repeat from * once. Ch 3, sc into top corner of floating block, ch 3, work 3 dc into top of turning ch.

Row 7: Repeat Row 4.

Row 8: Repeat Row 5.

Row 9: Repeat Row 6.

Rows 10–22: Repeat Rows 4–6 four times, then Row 4 once more, changing to B when 2 lps remain on hook at end of Row 22.

Row 23–25: With B, repeat Row 5, Row 6, and Row 4, changing to A when 2 lps remain on hook at end of Row 25.

Rows 26–40: With A, repeat Rows 5–6 once. Repeat Rows 4–6 four times. Repeat Row 4, changing to B when 2 lps remain on hook at end of Row 39.

Rows 41–46: With B, Repeat Rows 5–6 once. Repeat Rows 4–6 once. Repeat Row 4, changing to A when 2 lps remain on hook at end of Row 45.

Rows 47–58: With A, Repeat Rows 5–6 once. Repeat Rows 4–6 three times. Repeat Row 4, changing to B when 2 lps remain on hook at end of Row 57.

Rows 59–67: With B, Repeat Rows 5–6 once. Repeat Rows 4–6 twice. Repeat Row 4, changing to A when 2 lps remain on hook at end of Row 66.

Rows 68–76: With A, Repeat Rows 5–6 once. Repeat Rows 4–6 twice. Repeat Row 4, changing to B when 2 lps remain on hook at end of Row 75.

Rows 77–88: With B, repeat Rows 4–5 once. Repeat Rows 4–6 three times. Repeat Row 4, changing to A when 2 lps remain on hook at end of Row 87.

Rows 89–94: With A, Repeat Rows 4–5 once. Repeat Rows 4–6 once. Repeat Row 4, changing to B when 2 lps remain on hook at end of Row 93.

Rows 95–109: With B, Repeat Rows 4–5 once. Repeat Rows 4–6 four times. Repeat Row 4, changing to A when 2 lps remain on hook at end of Row 108.

Rows 110–112: Repeat Rows 5–6 once. Repeat Row 4. Do not change colors.

Row 113: Ch 1, turn. Sc in each of 3 dc, *3 sc into next ch-sp, sk next sc, 3 sc into next ch-3 sp, sc in each of next 3 dc, sk next ch-sp, sc in each of next 3 dc. Repeat from * once. 3 sc into next ch-3 sp, sk next sc, 3 sc into next ch-3 sp, sc in each of next 2 dc, 2 sc into top of turning ch. Total 37 sc.

Row 114: Ch 1, turn. Sc in each sc across. Total 37 sc. Fo.

Finishing

With tapestry needle, weave in ends. Lightly steam block scarf.

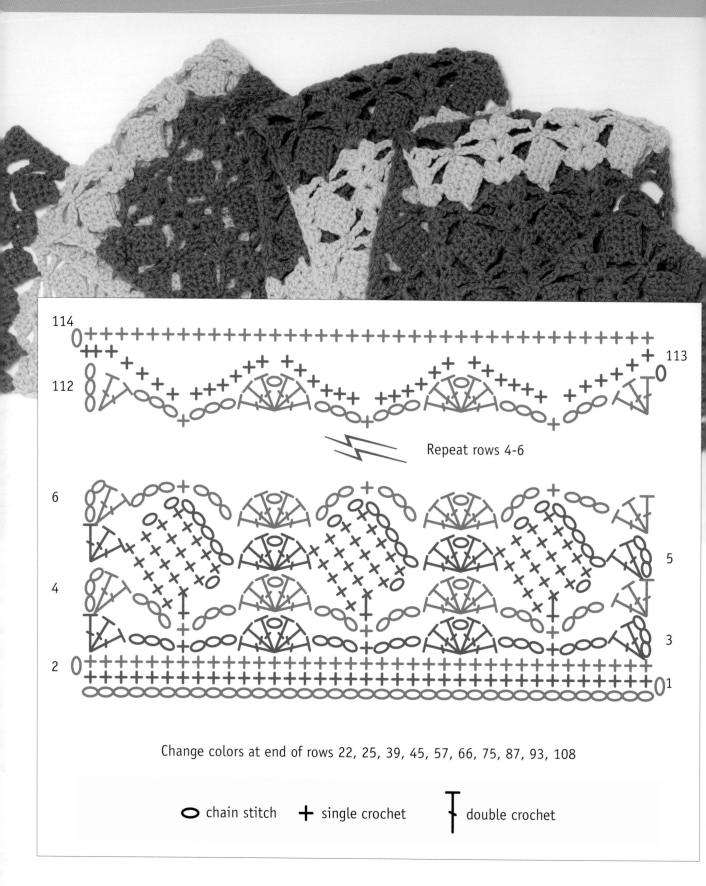

114

113

112

Repeat rows 4-6

6

5

4

3

2

1

Change colors at end of rows 22, 25, 39, 45, 57, 66, 75, 87, 93, 108

⬭ chain stitch   ✛ single crochet   ⊤ double crochet

Diamond Loop

Loop this scarf once, twice, or even three or four times to create a variety of interesting looks. The two-color motif uses mosaic crochet, in which one color is worked into stitches several rows below to cover the in-between color, for its distinctive lozenge shapes.

MEASUREMENTS

100 inches (254 centimeters) before seaming x 4 inches (10.2 centimeters)

MATERIALS

Abuelita Cotton, 100% cotton, 3.5 ounces/100 grams, 133 yards/126 meters

2

Fine

Color A: Grey (6549), 1 skein

Color B: Cream (6501), 1 skein

Crochet hook size G (4.25 mm) or size needed to obtain gauge

Tapestry needle

STITCHES AND ABBREVIATIONS

Chain (ch), chains (chs)

Double crochet (dc)

Fasten off (fo)

Half double crochet (hdc)

Loop (lp), loops (lps)

Right side (RS)

Single crochet (sc)

Skip (sk)

Slip stitch (sl st)

Stitch (st), stitches (sts)

Treble crochet (tr)

Wrong side (WS)

GAUGE

15 stitches and 7 rows in dc/4 inches (10.2 centimeters) blocked

For gauge swatch, ch 23. Last 3 chs count as first dc on Row 1.

Row 1: Dc into fourth ch from hook and in each ch across. Total 21 dc.

Row 2: Ch 3 (counts as dc), turn. Sk st at base of chs. Dc in each st across, ending with final dc in top of turning ch. Total 21 dc.

Repeat Row 2 until swatch measures at least 4.5 inches (11.4 centimeters)

Special Stitches

Lozenge Mosaic

With A, ch multiple of 12 plus 11. (For a practice swatch, ch 35.)

Row 1: Sc into second ch from hook and in each ch to end. (Swatch will have 34 sc.)

Row 2: Ch 1, turn. Sc in each st across, changing to B when 2 lps remain on hook in final sc. Cut A, leaving about a 4-inch tail.

> **NOTE** On the scarf, not the swatch, you will be sewing the ends together along this edge, so it is better to cut the yarn than to carry it along the seam. When you finish the project you can use the tails to sew the two sides together—lining up the colors perfectly. Leave the ends long enough to thread through a tapestry needle.

Row 3: Ch 3 (counts as dc). Turn. Sk sc at base of chs. Dc into next sc, hdc into next sc, sc into next sc. *Ch 2, sk 2 sc. Sc into next sc, hdc into next sc, dc into each of next 2 sc, tr into each of next 2 sc, dc into each of next 2 sc, hdc into next sc, sc into next sc. Repeat from * to last 6 sc. Ch 2, sk 2 sc. Sc into next sc, hdc into next sc, dc into each of the next 2 sc.

> **NOTE** This sets up the wave pattern. From the small end, each lozenge consists of ten stitches; on this row, it is sc, hdc, dc, dc, tr, tr, dc, dc, hdc, sc. The lozenges are separated by 2 chs (skipping over 2 stitches below). On the next row, you will amplify the effect by working tall stitches into the corresponding stitches below: sc will be worked into sc from the row below, hdc will be worked into hdc from the row below, and so on.

Row 4: Ch 3, turn. Sk dc at base of chs. Dc in next dc, hdc in next hdc, sc in next sc. *Ch 2, sk 2 ch. Sc into next sc, hdc into next hdc, dc into each of next 2 dc, tr into each of next 2 tr, dc into each of next 2 dc, hdc into next hdc, sc into next sc. Repeat from * to last 6 sc. Ch 2, sk 2 ch. Sc into next sc, hdc into next hdc, dc into next dc, dc into top of turning ch, changing to A when 2 lps remain on hook in final dc. Cut B, leaving a 4-inch tail. You will use this when seaming the ends of the scarf together.

Row 5: With A, ch 1, turn. Sc into each of next 4 sts. Sc into each of 2 unworked sc from 3 rows below, inserting hook from the front and pulling the lp up to the same height as the current row. *Sc into each of next 10 sts, sc into each of 2 unworked sc from 3 rows below. Repeat from * until 4 sts remain. Sc into each of next 3 sts, sc into top of turning ch.

Row 6: Ch 1, turn. Sc into each sc across, changing to B when 2 lps remain on hook in final st.

Row 7: With B, ch 1, turn. * Sc in sc, hdc in next sc, dc in each of next 2 sc, tr in each of next 2 sc, dc in each of next 2 sc, hdc in next sc, sc in next sc. Ch 2, sk 2 sc. Repeat from * across, omitting ch 2 at end of row.

Row 8: Ch 1. *Sc in sc, hdc in hdc, dc in each of next 2 dc, tr in each of next 2 tr, dc in each of next 2 dc, hdc in hdc, sc in sc. Ch 2, sk 2 ch below. Repeat from * across, omitting ch 2 at end of row. Change to A when 2 lps remain on hook.

Row 9: With A, Ch 1, turn. *Sc in each of the next 10 sts. Sc into each of 2 unworked sc from 3 rows below, inserting hook from the front and pulling the lp up to the same height as the current row. Repeat from * across, omitting 2 sc at end of row.

Repeat Rows 2–9.

Scarf

> **NOTE** The scarf is worked back and forth in long rows, then seamed to make a loop.

With A, ch 359.

> **NOTE** To make a shorter or longer scarf, subtract or add stitches in multiples of 12.

Row 1 (RS): Sc into second ch from hook and in each ch across. Total 358 sc.

Rows 2–17: Work Rows 2–9 of Lozenge Mosaic pattern twice.

Rows 18–22: Work Rows 2–6 of Lozenge Mosaic pattern. Fo.

Finishing

Lightly steam block scarf on WS. Do not weave in ends.

With RS together so WS is facing you, bring short ends of scarf together. Make sure loop is not twisted. Thread one of the tails onto a tapestry needle and stitch to the corresponding end of the scarf, being careful to match up the color. Weave in the end. Repeat the process with remaining tails. Keep seam as flat as possible; it should be almost invisible when you're done. Weave in any remaining ends. Invert the scarf so the RS is out.

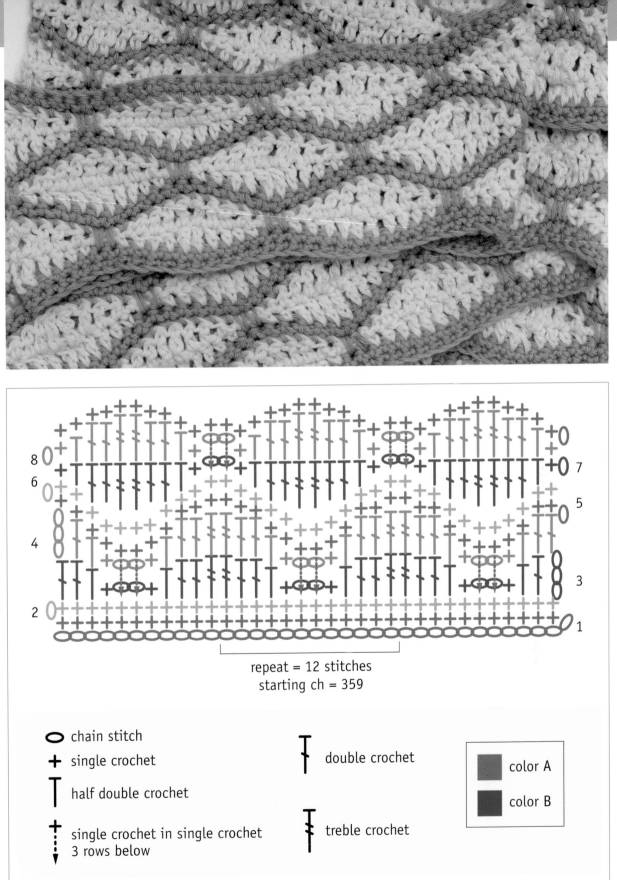

repeat = 12 stitches
starting ch = 359

O chain stitch
+ single crochet
T half double crochet
+ single crochet in single crochet
   3 rows below
† double crochet
‡ treble crochet

color A
color B

Champagne Goblets

SKILL LEVEL

■■■□
INTERMEDIATE

Luxurious, lustrous mohair is light and warm, perfect for an open-work scarf like this one. When using such a fine fiber, the trick is not to pull your stitches too tight, especially your starting chain. Make sure the yarn flows from the ball easily and is not pulling on your work. If this is the first time you have used mohair, get comfortable making chain stitches, single crochet, and double crochet before you start on the scarf.

The finished scarf weighs just one ounce and compresses to fist size, making it a great choice for travel.

MEASUREMENTS

62 inches (157.5 centimeters) by 5 inches (12.7 centimeters)

MATERIALS

Louet Kid Mohair, 70% kid mohair/30% nylon, 1.76 ounces/50 grams, 490 yards/448 meters

0

Lace

Champagne (87-1012-8): 1 skein

Crochet hook size H (5.00 mm)

Tapestry needle

STITCHES AND ABBREVIATIONS

Chain (ch), chains (chs)

Chain space (ch-sp)

Double crochet (dc)

Fasten off (fo)

Loop (lp), loops (lps)

Right side (RS)

Single crochet (sc)

Skip (sk)

Stitch (st), stitches (sts)

GAUGE

Gauge is flexible for this project. Suggested gauge is 13 stitches and 6 rows in dc/4 inches (10.2 centimeters), unblocked.

For gauge swatch, ch 25. Last 3 chs count as first dc on Row 1.

Row 1: Dc in fourth ch from hook and in each ch across. Total 23 dc.

Row 2: Ch 3 (counts as first dc), turn. Sk st at base of chs. Dc in each st across.

Rows 3–8: Repeat Row 2.

Scarf

> **NOTE** Photos show a DK yarn in bright teal so the stitches are easier to see than in pale, fuzzy mohair.

Side 1

Ch 194.

Row 1 (RS): Sc in second ch from hook. *Ch 3, sk 2 chs, sc in next ch. Repeat from * across.

Row 2: Ch 5, turn. Sc in ch-3 lp, ch 3, sc in next ch-3 lp, work 3 dc into next sc. *[Sc in next ch-3 lp, ch 3] 3 times, sc in next ch-3 lp, work 3 dc into next sc. Repeat from * until two ch-3 lps remain. Sc in next ch-3 lp, ch 3, sc in next ch-3 lp, ch 2, dc in sc.

Row 3: Ch 1, turn. Sc in dc, ch 3, sc in ch-3 lp. *[Ch 1, dc in next dc] 3 times, ch 1, [sc in next ch-3 lp, ch 3] twice, sc in next ch-3 lp. Repeat from * until one cluster of 3 dc remains. [Ch 1, dc in next dc] 3 times, ch 1, sc in next ch-3 lp, ch 3, sc in ch-5 lp.

Row 4: Ch 5, turn. *Sc in ch-3 lp, dc in next ch-1 sp, [2 dc in next dc, 2 dc under next ch-1 sp] twice, 2 dc in next dc, dc under next ch-1 sp, sc in next ch-3 lp, ch 3. Repeat from * across, changing final ch 3 to ch 2, dc into sc.

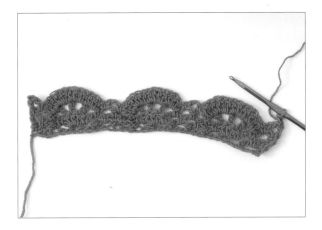

Row 5: Ch 1, turn. Sc in dc. *Ch 3, sk 2 dc, sc in next dc, ch 3, sk 3 dc, sc in the space between the just-skipped dc and the next dc, ch 3, sk 3 dc, sc in next dc, ch 3, sc in ch-3 lp. Repeat from * across.

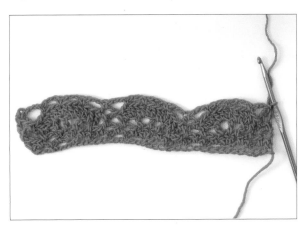

NOTE The center sc above the dc fan goes between two stitches, not into a stitch.

Row 6: Ch 3, turn. Dc in sc at base of chs. Sc in ch-3 lp. *[Ch 3, sc in next ch-3 lp] three times, 3 dc in sc, sc in ch-3 lp. Repeat from * until three ch-3 lps remain. [Ch 3, sc in next ch-3 lp] three times, work 2 dc in sc.

Row 7: Ch 4 (counts as dc and ch-1 sp), turn. Sk dc at base of chs. Dc in next dc, ch 1. *[Sc in next ch-3 lp, ch 3] twice. Sc in next ch-3 lp, [ch 1, dc in next dc] 3 times, ch 1. Repeat from * until three ch-3 lps remain. [Sc in next ch-3 lp, ch 3] twice, sc in next ch-3 lp, ch 1, dc in next dc, ch 1, dc into top of turning ch.

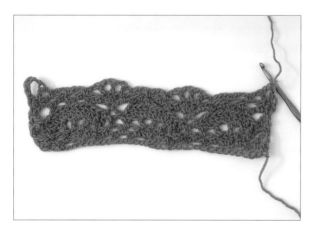

Row 8: Ch 3, turn. Dc at base of chs, 2 dc in ch-sp, 2 dc in next dc, dc in ch-1 sp. *Sc in ch-3 lp, ch 3, sc in next ch-3 lp. Dc in next ch-1 sp, [2 dc in next dc, 2 dc under next ch-1 sp] twice, 2 dc in next dc, dc under next ch-1 sp. Repeat from * across until two ch-3 lps remain. Sc in ch-3 lp, ch 3, sc in next ch-3 lp, Dc in ch-1 sp, 2 dc in next dc, 2 dc in next ch-1 sp, dc into top of turning ch.

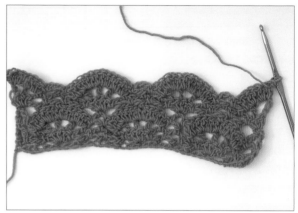

Side 2

With RS facing, join yarn in corner of foundation chain. Work Rows 1–8. Fo.

Trim on Short Sides

Row 1: With RS facing, join yarn in corner st. Sc 25 sts.

Row 2: Ch 1, turn. Sc in first sc. Sk 1 sc, 7 dc in next sc. *Sk 4 sc, 7 dc in next sc. Repeat from * until 2 sc remain. Sk 1 sc, sc in last sc. Fo.

Finishing

Using tapestry needle, weave in ends. Lightly steam block on WS if desired.

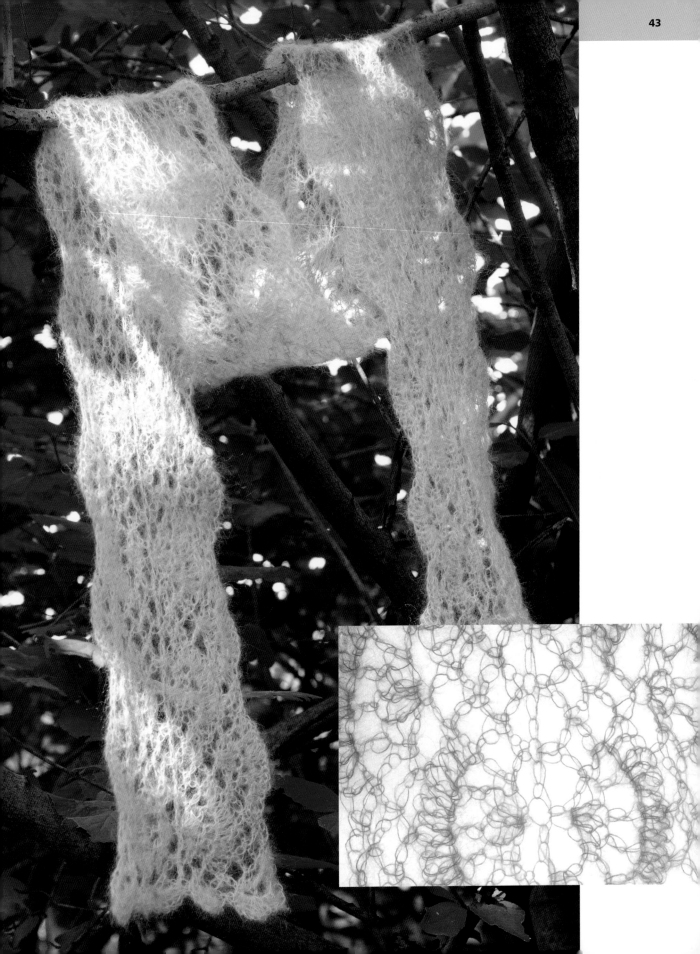

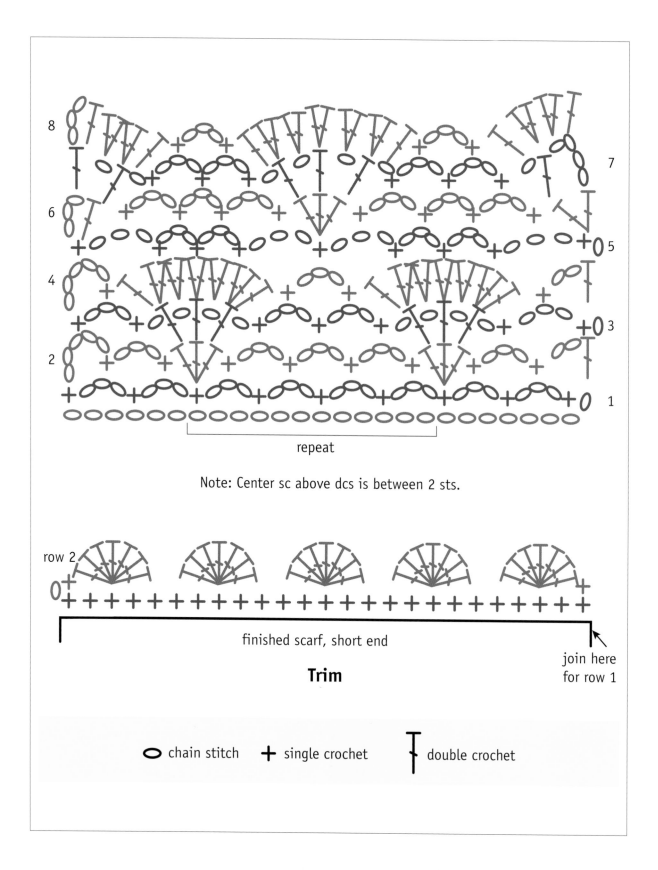

repeat

Note: Center sc above dcs is between 2 sts.

row 2

finished scarf, short end

join here
for row 1

Trim

○ chain stitch   + single crochet   ⊤ double crochet

Cactus Lace

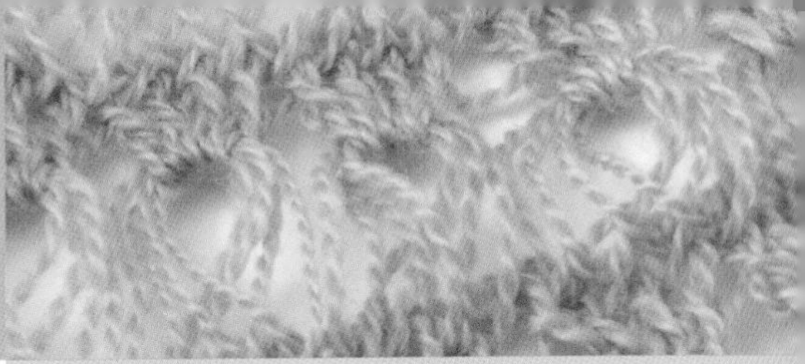

SKILL LEVEL

■■□□

EXPERIENCED

Broomstick lace, beautifully delicate, is worked in pairs of rows without turning; the right side is always facing you. The first row pulls up loops onto a knitting needle —or a broomstick, if you prefer!— and the next row closes the loops in groups, creating shapes like the eyes of peacock feathers.

MEASUREMENTS

67 inches (170.2 centimeters) by 3 inches (7.6 centimeters), plus 5 inches (12.7 centimeters) of fringe at each end

MATERIALS

SpaceCadet Creations Luna, 80% merino wool, 20% silk, 3.5 ounces/100 grams, 1300 yards/1189 meters; scarf uses approximately 275 yards (251.5 meters) of this yarn

Super Fine

Gilded Sage (110627-002): 1 skein

Crochet hook size E (3.50 mm) or size needed to obtain gauge

Knitting needle size 19 (15 mm)

Tapestry needle

6-inch (15.2 centimeter) piece of cardboard for making fringe

STITCHES AND ABBREVIATIONS

Chain (ch), chains (chs)

Double crochet (dc)

Fasten off (fo)

Loop (lp), loops (lps)

Right side (RS)

Single crochet (sc)

Skip (sk)

Stitch (st), stitches (sts)

Wrong side (WS)

Yarn over (yo)

GAUGE

23 stitches and 13 rows in dc/4 inches (10.2 centimeters), blocked

For gauge swatch, ch 32.

Row 1: Dc in fourth ch from hook (unworked chs count as dc). Dc in each ch across. Total 30 dc.

Row 2: Ch 3 (counts as dc). Turn. Sk st at base of chs. Dc in each st across, ending with dc in top of turning ch. Total 30 dc.

Repeat Row 2 until swatch measures at least 4.5 inches (11.4 centimeters).

Special Stitches

Broomstick Lace

Broomstick lace is worked in pairs of rows. The first row, known as the loop row, pulls up large loops and stores them on a knitting needle; the second row, called the crochet row, closes the loops in groups. The number of loops per group varies depending on the pattern. This pattern is worked in a multiple of 4 sts.

Both rows of broomstick lace are worked with the RS facing you. Do not turn your work. (When you get to the multiple rows of dc in the pattern, you will turn as is usual for dc rows.)

Begin with a multiple of 4 dc sts.

Loop Row: Using a crochet hook, pull up the loop on the hook until it is tall, then transfer it from the crochet hook to the knitting needle without twisting it. Hold your finished work and the working yarn behind the knitting needle. You may want to place the knitting needle under your arm or between your knees to keep it steady.

*Insert hook into the top of the next dc. (If you are right-handed, you will be moving from left to right; left-handers will be going from right to left.) Yo, pull up a lp and transfer it from the crochet hook to the knitting needle without twisting it. Make sure the loops are snug on the knitting needle, and that they do not cross over each other. Repeat from * across, pulling up final lp by inserting hook into top of turning ch.

Crochet Row: Do not turn. Slide all the loops off the needle, being careful not to pull on any of them. The loops are all live, but as long as you do not catch one and pull it, they will retain their shape.

You'll be working in groups of 4 sts. Insert the hook through the center of the first group of 4 loops. Yo, pull up a lp, being careful not to pull it too tight.

Ch 1 to anchor the group. (You only need this anchoring st for the first group on the row.) Ch 3. This counts as the first dc in this group.

Work 3 dc into same group of lps, right through the middle of the "peacock eye."

*Identify next group of 4 lps. Yo, insert hook through those 4 lps to begin dc. Complete the dc. Work 3 more dc into that same group of lps.

NOTE Sometimes a loop can droop down. Before you insert your crochet hook, make sure all of your loops are in line so you don't miss any. Check that the loops are not twisted and do not cross over each other.

Repeat from * across.

Scarf

Foundation: Ch 25.

Row 1 (RS): Sc in second ch from hook and in each ch across. Total 24 sc.

Row 2 (WS): Ch 3 (counts as dc), turn. Sk st at base of ch. Dc in each sc across. Total 24 dc.

Row 3: Repeat Row 2.

Row 4: Do not turn. Work loop row of broomstick lace.

Row 5: Do not turn. Work crochet row of broomstick lace.

Row 6–9: Repeat Rows 4 and 5 twice.

Row 10: Ch 3 (counts as dc), turn. Sk st at base of chs. Dc in each st across, ending with dc in top of ch-3. Total 24 dc.

Row 11: Repeat Row 10.

Rows 12–123: Repeat Rows 4–11 fourteen times. Fo.

Finishing
With tapestry needle, weave in ends. Lightly steam block scarf on WS.

Fringe
There are 23 sets of fringe on each end. Each set has one strand folded over to make two strands.

Loosely wrap yarn around a piece of cardboard 46 times. Cut the bottom edge of the yarn to make 46 strands.

Take one strand of yarn and fold it in half. With RS of scarf facing you, slip the crochet hook through the space between stitches from the back of the scarf to the front. Pull the folded end of the fringe through from front to back. Slip both cut ends through the folded part of the fringe. Pull taut. Attach fringe in each of the 23 spaces across the bottom and across the top of the scarf.

Lightly steam block the fringe. Trim the fringe so it is even, approximately 5 inches (12.7 centimeters) long.

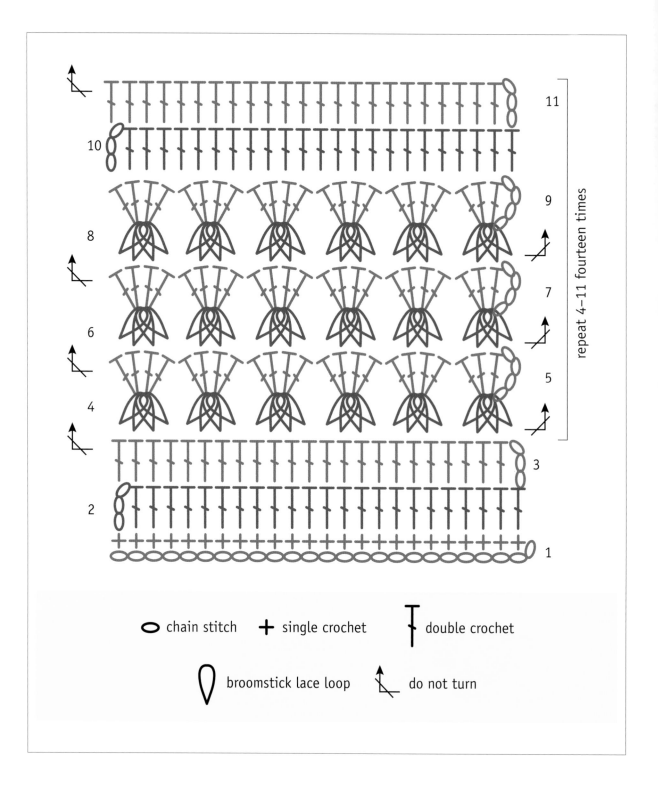

11

10

9

8

7

6

5

4

3

2

1

repeat 4–11 fourteen times

○ chain stitch   ✚ single crochet   ┳ double crochet

◯ broomstick lace loop   ↰ do not turn

Grecian Ladders

SKILL LEVEL

■■□□

EASY

Tunisian crochet's features lend themselves beautifully to structural, almost architectural, patterns. This one looks like Greek columns.

MEASUREMENTS

60 (152.4 centimeters) by 2.75 inches (7.0 centimeters)

MATERIALS

Kangaroo Dyer High Twist Poet Seat Yarn, 80% blue-faced Leicester wool, 20% nylon, 4 ounces/114 grams, 400 yards/365.7 meters; project uses approximately 200 yards of this yarn.

Super Fine

Echinacea, 1 skein

Tunisian crochet hook size I (5.5 mm) or size needed to obtain gauge

Crochet hook size H (5.0 mm) or one size smaller than Tunisian hook

Tapestry needle

STITCHES AND ABBREVIATIONS

Chain (ch), chains (chs)

Fasten off (fo)

Loop (lp), loops (lps)

Right side (RS)

Single crochet (sc)

Skip (sk)

Slip stitch (sl st)

Stitch (st)

Tunisian simple stitch (Tss)

Wrong side (WS)

Yarn over (yo)

GAUGE

Gauge is flexible for this project. Suggested gauge is 22 sts and 10 rows/4 inches (10.2 centimeters) in pattern, blocked.

For gauge swatch, ch 26. Work in pattern through Row 15.

Scarf

Ch 14.

Row 1 forward (RS): Insert hook in second ch from hook, yo, pull up lp. *Insert hook into next ch, yo, pull up lp. Repeat from * across. Total 14 lps on hook. Do not turn.

Row 1 return: Yo, pull through 1 lp. *Yo, pull through 2 lps. Repeat from * across until 1 lp remains on hook.

NOTE Work every return pass this way.

Row 2: Sk first vertical bar. *Yo. Tss in each of next 3 sts. (There is only 1 yo before a set of three Tss, not before each st.) Take the yo you made before the 3 Tss and pull it over those 3 sts and off the hook. This will create a horizontal bar atop 3 sts. Repeat from * across until 1 st remains. Tss in final st. Return.

NOTE The last stitch of the forward pass is always a Tss. Work it into the final vertical bar and the horizontal thread that runs behind it for stability.

pull through both lps (sc made). Repeat from * across, working 2 sc in the corner so it lies flat. Sc evenly down side, across bottom, and up other side of scarf. Join to first st with sl st. Fo.

Finishing

With tapestry needle, weave in ends. Lightly steam block on WS if desired.

Repeat Row 2 until scarf measures 59.5 inches (151.1 centimeters).

Final Row and Border: Change to regular crochet hook one size smaller than Tunisian hook. Sk first vertical bar. *Insert hook in next vertical bar as for Tss, yo, pull up lp, yo,

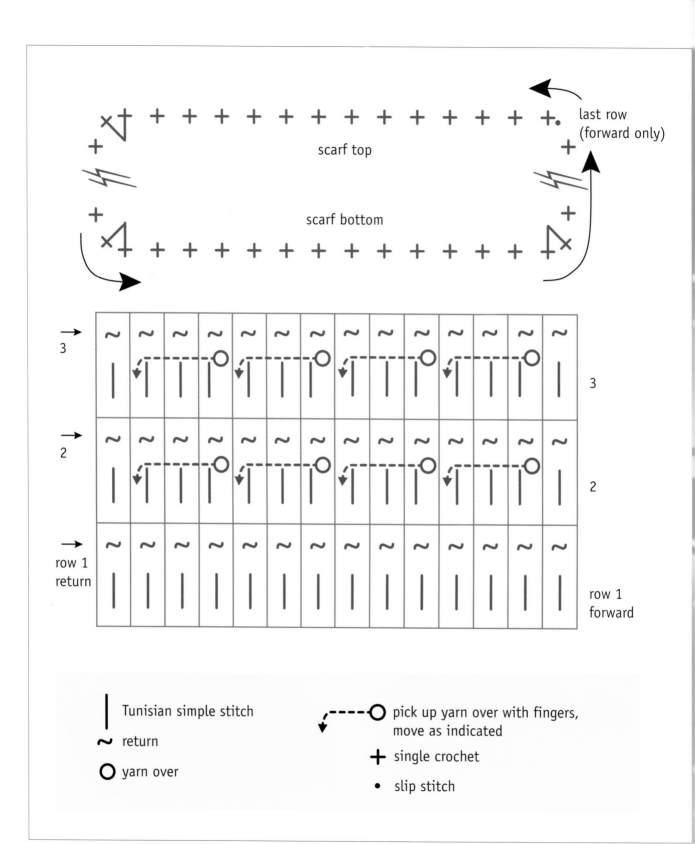

last row
(forward only)

scarf top

scarf bottom

3

2

row 1
return

row 1
forward

| Tunisian simple stitch

~ return

O yarn over

- - - - O pick up yarn over with fingers,
move as indicated

+ single crochet

• slip stitch

Premium Cable

One stately cable climbs up this attractive Tunisian crochet scarf, made with variegated Amazing from Lion Brand. Tunisian knit stitches form the side border, while the Tunisian purl stitches on either side of the cable create a recessed background to frame it.

If you have been hesitant to try cables, put your reluctance aside and give it a try. Follow the step-by-step instructions and you'll discover that it's not as hard as it looks!

MEASUREMENTS

65 inches (165.1 centimeters) by 4 inches (10.2 centimeters).

MATERIALS

Lion Brand Amazing, 53% wool, 47% acrylic, 147 yards/135 meters, 1.75 ounces/50 grams

Medium

Pink Sands (#207), 3 skeins

Tunisian crochet hook size K (6.5 mm) or size needed to obtain gauge

Cable needle (size does not matter as long as you can slide your stitches onto it without stretching them)

Tapestry needle

STITCHES AND ABBREVIATIONS

Chain (ch), chains (chs)

Fasten off (fo)

Loop (lp), loops (lps)

RS (right side)

Single crochet (sc)

Skip (sk)

Stitch (st), stitches (sts)

Tunisian knit stitch (Tks)

Tunisian purl stitch (Tps)

Tunisian simple stitch (Tss)

Yarn over (yo)

GAUGE

18 stitches and 13 rows in pattern/4 inches (10.2 centimeters), blocked.

For gauge swatch, work in pattern through Row 13. Gently block. If your gauge is accurate, use gauge swatch as the first 13 rows of the scarf.

Special Stitch

Tunisian Purl Stitch (Tps)

Forward: Bring yarn to front of work.

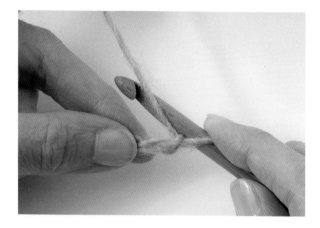

Insert hook as instructed.

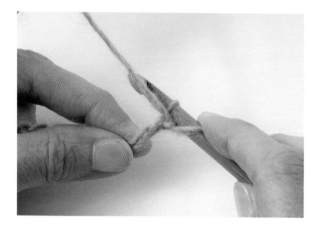

Bring the yarn toward you in front of the stitch, then back under the hook.

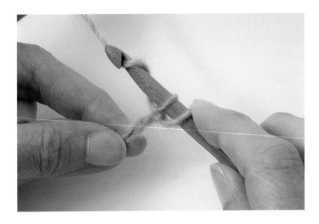

Yo, pull up a lp. You will see the characteristic "purl bump" in front. Each st adds 1 lp to hook.

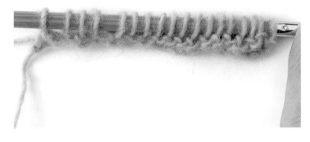

Return: Do not turn. Yo, pull through 1 lp, *Yo, pull through 2 lps. Repeat from * until 1 lp remains on hook.

Scarf

Chain 18.

Row 1 forward (RS): *Bring yarn to front of hook as for Tps, insert hook in second ch from hook, yo, pull up lp. Repeat from * to last ch, Tss in last ch. Total 18 lps on hook.

Row 1 return: Do not turn. Yo, pull through 1 lp. *Yo, pull through 2 lps. Repeat from * until 1 lp remains on hook.

NOTE Work every return pass this way.

Row 2: Sk first vertical bar. Tps in each Tps to last st. Tss in final st, inserting hook into vertical bar and horizontal bar that runs behind it for stability. Return.

Row 3: Repeat Row 2.

Row 4: Sk first vertical bar. Tks in each of next 2 sts, Tps in each of next 3 sts, Tks in each of next 6 sts, Tps in each of next 3 sts, Tks in each of next 2 sts, Tss in final st. Return.

Row 5: Repeat Row 4.

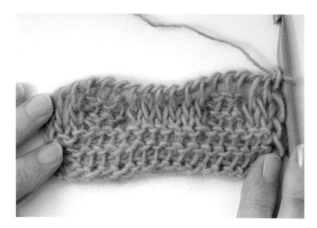

Row 6 (begin cable): Sk first vertical bar. Tks in each of next 2 sts, Tps in each of next 3 sts. Tks in each of next 3 sts, then slide those lps onto cable needle without twisting them. Hold cable needle to front of work.

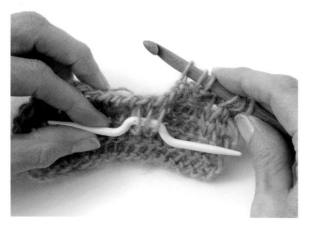

Tks in each of next 3 sts (keep these fairly loose so cable does not twist too much).

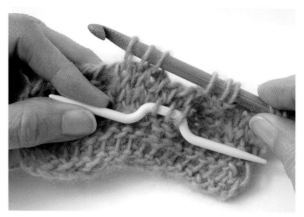

Slide the sts from the cable needle back onto crochet hook without twisting them. Keep them in order. The cable section will feel tight, but will loosen up on the return pass.

Tps in each of next 3 sts, Tks in each of next 2 sts, Tss in final st. Return, spreading out the lps on your hook so you can clearly see them on the return. Make sure you do not pull through 3 lps by mistake.

> **NOTE** In Row 7, it can be hard to see the back part of the cable. Use your fingers to spread out the stitches. Make sure to work the back 3 sts first, then the ones in front. Keep the stitches in order without twisting them.

Row 7: Sk first vertical bar. Tks in each of next 2 sts, Tps in each of next 3 sts, Tks in each of next 6 sts, Tps in each of next 3 sts, Tks in each of next 2 sts, Tss in final st. Return.

Row 8: Sk first vertical bar. Tks in each of next 2 sts, Tps in each of next 3 sts, Tks in each of next 6 sts, Tps in each of next 3 sts, Tks in each of next 2 sts, Tss in final st. Return.

Row 9: Repeat Row 8.

Repeat Rows 6–9 until scarf measures approximately 64 inches (160.6 cm).

Next 2 Rows: Sk first vertical bar. Tps in each st across to last st, Tss in last st. Return.

Final Row: Sk first vertical bar. *Bring yarn to front of work as for Tps, insert hook behind next vertical bar as for Tps, yo, pull up lp, yo, pull through 2 lps (sc made). Repeat from * across to last st, insert hook in last st as for Tss, yo, pull up lp, yo, pull through 2 lps (sc made). Fo.

Finishing

With tapestry needle, weave in ends. Lightly steam block scarf.

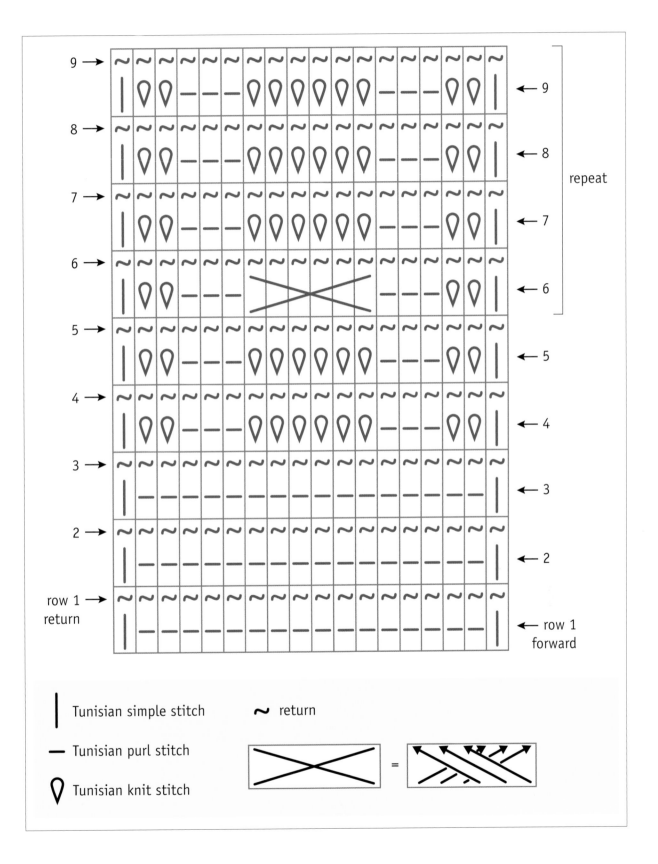

	Tunisian simple stitch	~	return

— Tunisian purl stitch

◊ Tunisian knit stitch

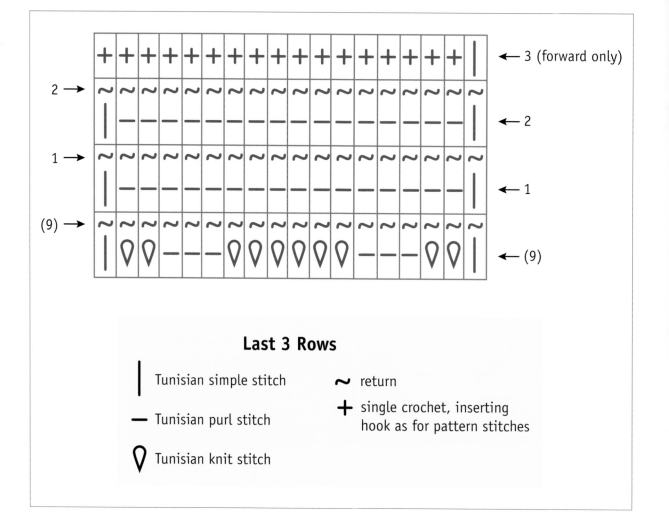

← 3 (forward only)

2 →

← 2

1 →

← 1

(9) →

← (9)

Last 3 Rows

| Tunisian simple stitch

~ return

— Tunisian purl stitch

+ single crochet, inserting hook as for pattern stitches

◊ Tunisian knit stitch

Ambrosia

Working on the diagonal in sets of blocks gives this scarf a unique arrangement of stitches that seem to go horizontally and vertically in one row. The scarf starts at the point and increases until it is six blocks wide. Once it is the desired length, it is fastened off, leaving a straight edge. A second, small piece is also worked from the point until it is six blocks wide, then attached to the straight edge of the scarf to create symmetrical points.

MEASUREMENTS

61 inches (154.9 centimeters) by 3.75 inches (9.5 centimeters)

MATERIALS

Blue Heron Silk Merino Lace, 50% silk, 50% merino wool, 4 ounces/113.4 grams, 1200 yards/ 1097.28 meters

Lace

Peaches & Cream, 1 skein; project uses approximately 250 yards of this yarn

Crochet hook size K (6.5 mm) or size needed to obtain gauge

Tapestry needle

STITCHES AND ABBREVIATIONS

Chain (ch), chains (chs)

Double crochet (dc)

Fasten off (fo)

Slip stitch (sl st)

GAUGE

5 blocks in each direction/4 inches (10.2 centimeters), unblocked

For gauge swatch, work pattern through Row 7.

If your gauge is accurate, you can use this as the start of your scarf.

Scarf

The Main Part of the Scarf

Ch 6. Last 3 chs will count as first dc in next block.

Row 1: Dc in fourth ch from hook and in each of next two chs. Total 4 dc (including turning ch). This counts as one block.

> **NOTE** Each row of blocks has one more block than the previous row. For example, Row 2 adds 2 blocks arranged in a stepwise fashion. Row 3 adds 3 blocks, Row 4 adds 4 blocks.

Row 2: Ch 6. Work 1 dc in fourth, fifth, and sixth ch from hook. Flip up the first block so the dc stitches are perpendicular to the ones you just made. Sl st into the space below the top dc (like under the top rung of a ladder) to connect the blocks. Ch 3 (counts as dc), work 3 dc into space below the top dc where you made the sl st. Two blocks made on this row for a total of 3 blocks.

The tapestry needle in the part of Block 1 that you will flip to be adjacent to where your hook is now.

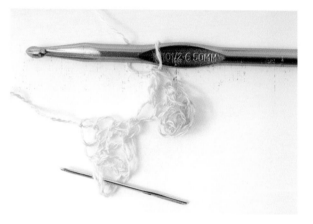

The block after it has been flipped. The needle shows where you will work the sl st.

The two blocks joined by a slip stitch.

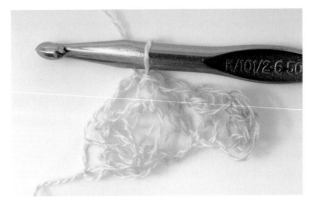

The completed Row 2.

Row 3: Ch 6. Work 1 dc in fourth, fifth, and sixth ch from hook. Flip up the completed three blocks so the dc stitches are alongside and perpendicular to the ones you just made. *Sl st into the space below the top dc in the adjacent block. Ch 3 (counts as dc), work 3 dc into space below the top dc where you made the sl st. Repeat from * to end of row. Three blocks made on this row for a total of 6 blocks.

Row 4: Ch 6. Work 1 dc in fourth, fifth, and sixth ch. Flip up the completed blocks so the dc stitches are perpendicular to the ones you just made. *Sl st into the space below the top dc in the adjacent block. Ch 3 (counts as dc). 3 dc into space below the top dc where you made the sl st. Repeat from * to end. Four blocks made on this row for a total of 10 blocks.

Row 5: Repeat Row 4. Five blocks made on this row for a total of 15 blocks.

Row 6: Repeat Row 4. Six blocks made on this row for a total of 21 blocks.

NOTE Each row will now have six blocks. To keep the scarf the same width as it gets longer, you will only add a block at the end of each odd-numbered row and at the beginning of each even-numbered row.

Row 7: Ch 3, turn. This group of 3 chs will nestle along the side of the scarf. Sl st in top dc of the block those chs are alongside. Ch 3 (counts as dc). 3 dc into space below the top dc where you made the sl st. *Sl st into the space below the top dc in the adjacent block. Ch 3 (counts as dc). 3 dc into space below the top dc where you made the sl st. Repeat from * 5 times.

Row 8: Ch 6. Work 1 dc in fourth, fifth, and sixth ch. Flip up the completed blocks so the dc stitches are perpendicular to the ones you just made. *Sl st into the space be-

low the top dc in the adjacent block. Ch 3 (counts as dc). 3 dc into space below the top dc where you made the sl st. Repeat from * 4 times. Sl st into the space below the top dc in the adjacent block. Do not add another block at the end of this row.

Repeat Rows 7 and 8 until scarf measures approximately 54 inches (137.2 centimeters), ending with Row 7. Fo.

The Second Point of the Scarf

Leaving at least a 5-inch tail, work pattern Rows 1–6. Fo.

Line up the straight edge of the triangle with the straight edge of the main part of the scarf. The ends of the scarf should be symmetrical. Thread a tapestry needle with the long tail you started with. Sew the small piece onto the main part of scarf. Do not pull too tight; try to maintain similar tension to that in the crocheted pieces. Knot the end so it does not unravel.

Finishing

Weave in ends. Lightly steam block if desired.

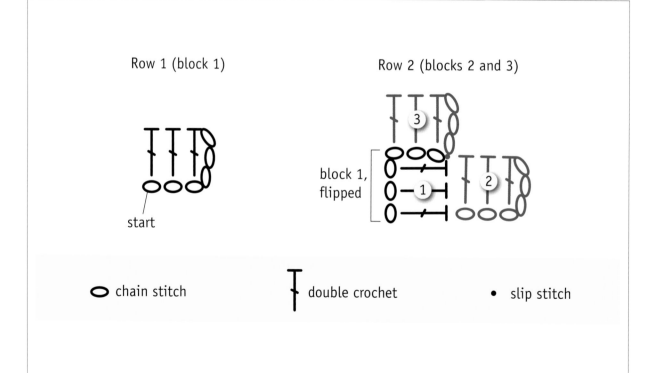

Row 1 (block 1)   Row 2 (blocks 2 and 3)

block 1, flipped

start

○ chain stitch   ⊤ double crochet   • slip stitch

Row 3 (blocks 4, 5, and 6)

Row 4 (blocks 7, 8, 9, and 10)

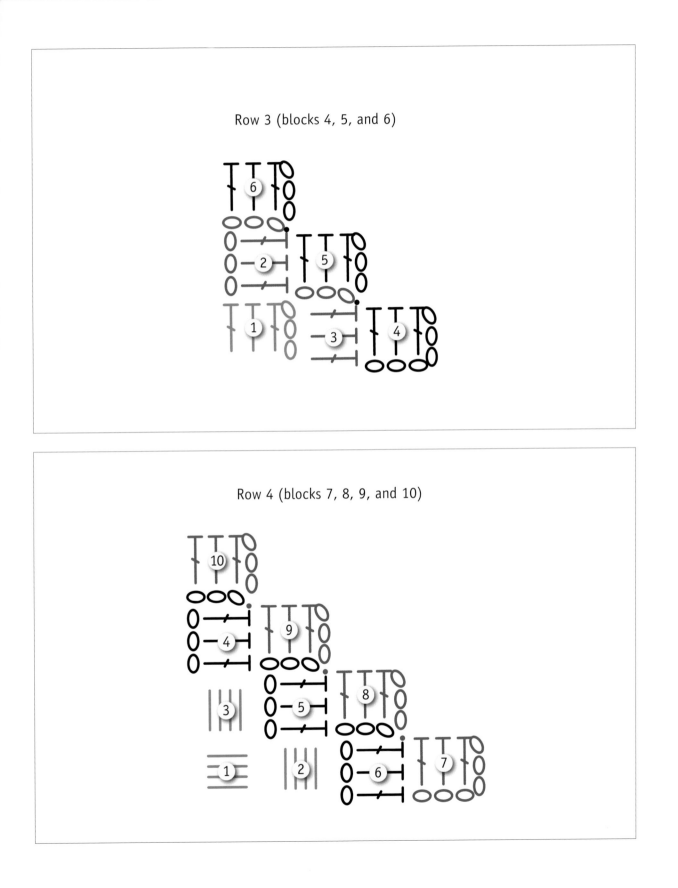

Row 5 (blocks 11, 12, 13, 14, and 15)

Row 6 (blocks 16, 17, 18, 19, 20, and 21)

Row 7 and all subsequent odd-numbered rows

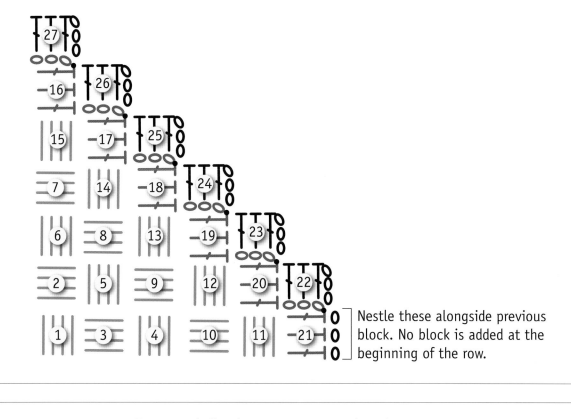

Nestle these alongside previous block. No block is added at the beginning of the row.

Row 8 and all subsequent even-numbered rows

Stop here; do not add another block at the end of the row.

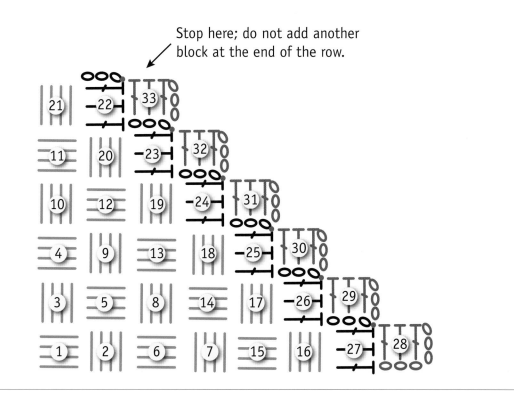

Classic Plaid

SKILL LEVEL

INTERMEDIATE

Tunisian simple stitch provides a linear structure that lends itself well to embellishment. In this scarf, red, white, and black yarn are worked with the main tan color to create the horizontally striped background. Those same accent colors are chained onto the scarf in vertical lines to complete the plaid look. I used the loop stitch—a variation of single crochet in which a long loop is pulled up—and then cut the loops to make a thick, short fringe to finish off this classic scarf.

MEASUREMENTS

51 inches (129.5 centimeters) by 6.5 inches (16.5 centimeters) plus 1.5 (3.8 centimeters) inches of fringe at each end

MATERIALS

Abuelita Baby Merino Lace, 100% merino wool, 3.5 ounces/100 grams, 420 yards/384 meters

Super Fine

Color A, 6988, desert flower, 1 skein

Color B, 9000, midnight black, 1 skein

Color C, 3, raw white, 1 skein

Color D, 1 3399, red, 1 skein

Tunisian crochet hook size H (5.00 mm) or size needed to obtain gauge

Crochet hook size G (4.25 mm) or one size smaller than Tunisian hook

Tapestry needle

STITCHES AND ABBREVIATIONS

Chain (ch), chains (chs)

Fasten off (fo)

Loop (lp), loops (lps)

Loop stitch (lp st)

Right side (RS)

Single crochet (sc)

Skip (sk)

Space (sp), spaces (sps)h

Stitch (st), stitches (sts)

Tunisian simple stitch (Tss)

Wrong side (WS)

Yarn over (yo)

Special Stitch

Loop Stitch (lp st)

1. Insert hook as for sc.
2. Using a finger of your yarn hand, pull up the yarn to form a lp approximately 1 inch (2.5 centimeters) tall.

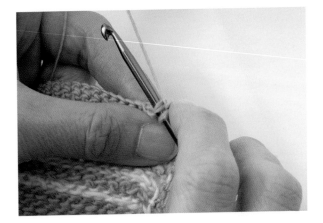

3. Put hook behind both both strands of the lp near the base and pull up both strands, leaving the loopy end sticking out the back.

4. Release lp from your finger. Using working yarn (not tall lp), yo, pull through all 3 lps.

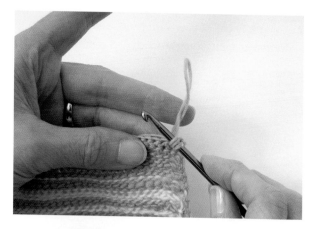

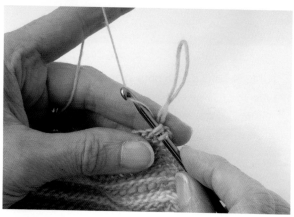

GAUGE

22 stitches and 16 rows in Tss/4 inches (10.2 centimeters), blocked

For gauge swatch, ch 26.

Row 1 forward: Insert hook in second ch from hook, yo, pull up lp. *Insert hook in next ch, yo, pull up lp. Repeat from * across. Total 26 lps on hook. Do not turn.

Row 1 return: Yo, pull through 1 lp. *Yo, pull through 2 lps. Repeat from * until 1 lp remains on hook.

> **NOTE** Work all return passes this way.

Row 2: Sk first vertical bar. *Tss in next vertical bar. Repeat from * across. Total 26 lps on hook. Return.

Repeat Row 2 until swatch measures 4.5 inches (11.4 centimeters).

Scarf

With A, ch 40.

Row 1 forward (RS): Insert hook in second ch from hook, yo, pull up lp. *Insert hook in next ch, yo, pull up lp. Repeat from * across. Total 40 lps on hook. Do not turn.

Row 1 return: Yo, pull through 1 lp. *Yo, pull through 2 lps. Repeat from * until 1 lp remains on hook.

> **NOTE** Work all return passes this way.

Row 2: Sk first vertical bar. *Tss in next vertical bar. Repeat from * across. Total 40 lps on hook. Return.

> **NOTE** Work the last Tss into the vertical bar and the horizontal strand behind it for stability.

Rows 3–11: Repeat Row 2.

Row 12: Continuing with A, work forward pass as usual. Drop A, pick up B by looping it over the hook, leaving approximately a 4-inch tail. Return with B.

Row 13: With B, work forward pass as usual. Drop B, pick up A. Return with A.

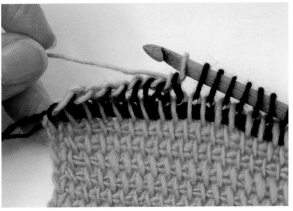

Rows 14–15: Repeat Rows 12 and 13. At end of Row 15 forward, cut B, leaving long tail. Return with A.

Rows 16–23: With A, repeat Row 2.

Row 24: Continuing with A, work forward pass as usual. Drop A, pick up C. Return with C.

Row 25: With C, work forward pass as usual. Drop C, pick up A. Return with A.

Rows 26–27: Repeat Rows 24–25. At end of Row 25 forward, cut C, leaving long tail. Return with A.

Rows 28–32: With A, repeat Row 2.

Rows 29–38: Repeat Rows 12–13.

Rows 39–41: With A, Repeat Row 2.

Row 42: Continuing with A, work forward pass as usual. Drop A, pick up D. Return with D.

Row 43: With D, work forward pass as usual. Drop D, pick up A. Return with A. At end of row 43 forward, cut D, leaving a long tail. Return with A.

Rows 44–51: Repeat Row 2.

Rows 52–55: Repeat Rows 42–43.

Rows 56–65: Repeat Row 2.

Rows 66–67: Repeat Rows 24–25.

Row 68: Repeat Row 2.

Rows 69–72: Repeat Rows 24–25.

Rows 73–78: Repeat Row 2.

Rows 79–84: Repeat Rows 12–13.

Rows 85–95: Repeat Row 2.

Rows 96–107: Repeat Rows 42–43.

Rows 108–111: Repeat Row 2.

Rows 112–117: Repeat Rows 24–25.

Rows 118–120: Repeat Rows 12–13.

Rows 121–133: Repeat Row 2.

Rows 134–137: Repeat Rows 24–25.

Rows 138–142: Repeat Row 2.

Rows 143–150: Repeat Rows 12–13.

Rows 151–157: Repeat Row 2.

Rows 158–161: Repeat Rows 42–43.

Rows 162–163: Repeat Row 2.

Rows 164–173: Repeat Rows 24–25.

Rows 174–177: Repeat Row 2.

Rows 178–179: Repeat Rows 24–25.

Rows 180–182: Repeat Row 2.

Rows 183–194: Repeat Rows 12–13.

Rows 195–206: Repeat Row 2.

Row 207: Switch to regular crochet hook one size smaller than your Tunisian hook. Sk first vertical bar. Insert hook in next vertical bar as for Tss, yo, pull up lp, yo, pull through both lps (sc made). Sc in each vertical bar across, entering stitch as for Tss. Work 2 sc in corner so it lies flat. Continue working sc evenly down side, across bottom, and up other side. Join to first st with sl st. Fo.

Finishing

Finishing Main Scarf

With tapestry needle, weave in ends. Gently steam block scarf on the WS, making sure sides and ends are straight and corners are neat.

Embellishment

With RS of scarf facing you, and using B, insert hook from front to back between third and fourth vertical bars on first row of scarf, pull up a lp (yarn ball is held behind the work). *Insert hook in next row up, exactly above the first st, pull up lp, and pull that lp through lp on hook (sl st made). Repeat from * up to the top edge of scarf. Fo.

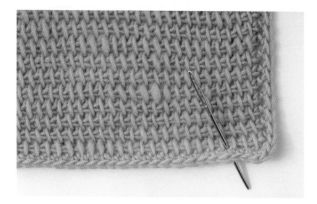

The needle shows where to begin the first embellishment row.

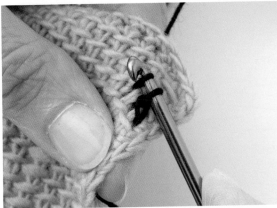

Move 7 sts to the left, repeat embellishment with D.
Move 2 sts to the left, repeat embellishment with C.
Move 13 sts to the left, repeat embellishment with B.
Move 8 sts to the left, repeat embellishment with C.
Move 5 sts to the left, repeat embellishment with D.
With tapestry needle, weave in ends.

Fringe

Row 1: With RS facing, use the regular crochet hook to attach color A in top right corner of scarf. Sc in each st across.

Row 2: Ch 1, turn. Work a lp st in each sc across. Fo. Cut loops to create fringe.

Repeat on other end of scarf.

Finishing Fringe

With tapestry needle, weave in ends where you started and ended the fringe. Lightly steam block fringe, then trim it so it is even.

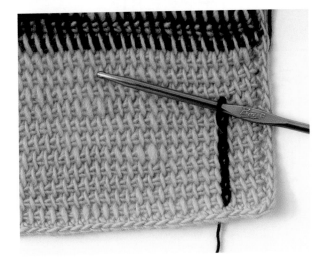

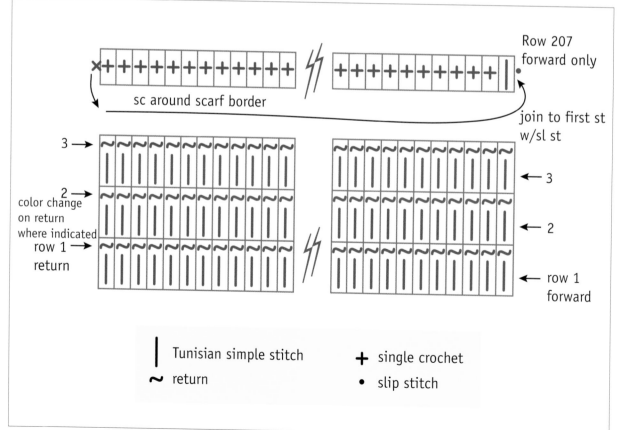

Row 207
forward only

sc around scarf border

join to first st
w/sl st

3

2
color change
on return
where indicated
row 1
return

3

2

row 1
forward

| Tunisian simple stitch   + single crochet

~ return   • slip stitch

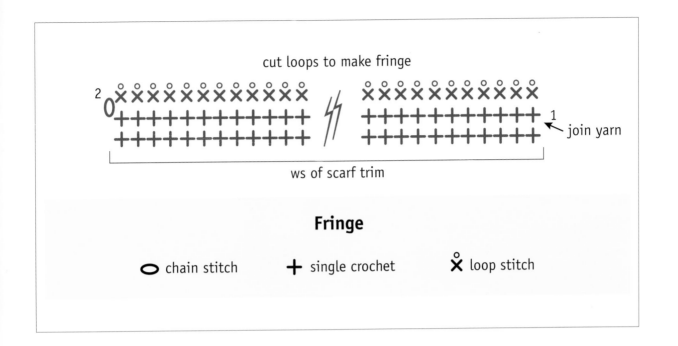

cut loops to make fringe

ws of scarf trim

join yarn

Fringe

⬭ chain stitch   ✚ single crochet   ⫶X loop stitch

Catch a Weave

SKILL LEVEL

■■■□

INTERMEDIATE

Basketweave stitch always makes me feel like I'm getting away with something: it looks so complex, yet it's just front and back post double crochet stitches (some people call them "raised" instead of "post" stitches; it's the same thing). Structured fringe maintains the linear style of this scarf.

MEASUREMENTS

60 inches (152.4 centimeters) by 4 inches (10.2 centimeters), plus 4 inches (10.2 centimeters) of fringe at each end

MATERIALS

Lanaloft from Brown Sheep Company, Inc., 100% wool, 3.5 ounces/100 grams, 160 yards/146 meters

4

Medium

Bridal Rose (LL09W), 3 skeins

Crochet hook size J (6.0 mm) or size needed to obtain gauge

Tapestry needle

STITCHES AND ABBREVIATIONS

Back post double crochet (bpdc)

Chain (ch), chains (chs)

Double crochet (dc)

Fasten off (fo)

Front post double crochet (fpdc)

Half double crochet (hdc)

Loop (lp), loops (lps)

Right side (RS)

Single crochet (sc)

Skip (sk)

Slip stitch (sl st)

Stitch (st), stitches (sts)

Wrong side (WS)

Yarn over (yo)

GAUGE

Gauge is flexible for this project. Suggested gauge is 12 stitches and 7 rows in dc/4 inches (10.2 centimeters), unblocked.

For gauge swatch, ch 21. Final 3 chs count as first dc on next row.

NOTE Gauge swatch is done in regular double crochet stitches, not post stitches.

Row 1: Dc in 4th ch from hook and in each ch across. Total 19 dc.

Row 2: Ch 3 (counts as dc), turn. Sk st at base of chs. Dc in each dc across, ending with dc in top of turning ch. Total 19 dc.

Rows 3–8: Repeat Row 2.

Special Stitches

NOTE Post stitches are worked in the spaces around a stitch.

Back Post Double Crochet (Bpdc)

The hook should start and end at the *back* of the work. Tilt the finished part of the work away from you to make it easier to see where to put the hook. Yo, insert hook from right to left around the post of the stitch below. Yo, pull up lp (3 lps on hook). Yo, pull through 2 lps, yo, pull through remaining 2 lps.

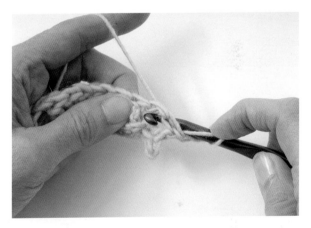

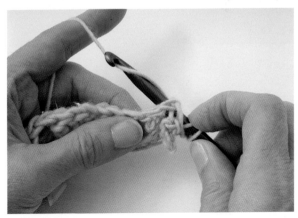

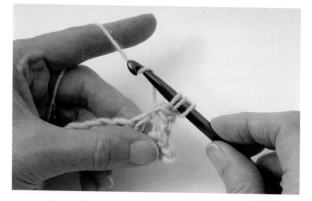

Front Post Double Crochet (Fpdc)

The hook should start and end at the *front* of the work. Tilt the finished part of the work toward you to make it easier to see where to put the hook. Yo, insert hook from right to left around the post of the stitch below. You, pull up lp (3 lps on hook). Yo, pull through 2 lps, yo, pull through remaining 2 lps.

Scarf

Foundation: Ch 15.

Row 1 (RS): Sc in second ch from hook and in each ch across. Total 14 sc.

Row 2 (WS): Ch 1. Turn. Do not sk sc at base of ch. Sc in each sc across. Total 14 sc.

Row 3 (commence pattern): Ch 2. Turn. Sk st at base of chs. Fpdc around each of next 4 sts, bpdc around each of next 4 sts, fpdc around each of next 4 sts. Hdc in final st.

> **NOTE** Make sure you are go around the posts of the stitches on Row 2, not Row 1.

Row 4: Ch 2, turn. You'll notice that the fpdc stitches from previous row now look like bpdc. Sk st at base of chs. Bpdc around each of next 4 sts, fpdc around each of next 4 sts, bpdc around each of next 4 sts. Hdc into top of turning ch.

Row 5: Ch 2, turn. Sk st at base of chs. Fpdc around each of next 4 sts, bpdc around each of net 4 sts, fpdc around each of next 4 sts. Hdc into top of turning ch.

Row 6: Ch 2, turn. Sk st at base of chs. Bpdc around each of next 4 sts, fpdc around each of next 4 sts, bpdc around each of next 4 sts. Hdc into top of turning ch.

> **NOTE** Row 7 starts the alternate blocks for the basketweave. Instead of reinforcing the pattern like you did on Rows 4–6, you are going to switch the pattern to create horizontal ridges above vertical, and vertical above horizontal.

Row 7: Ch 2, turn. Sk st at base of chs. Bpdc around each of next 4 sts, fpdc around each of next 4 sts, bpdc around each of next 4 sts. Hdc into top of turning ch.

Row 8: Ch 2, turn. Sk st at base of chs. Fpdc around each of next 4 sts, bpdc around each of next 4 sts, fpdc around each of next 4 sts. Hdc into top of turning ch.

Row 9: Ch 2, turn. Sk st at base of chs. Bpdc around each of next 4 sts, fpdc around each of next 4 sts, bpdc around each of next 4 sts. Hdc into top of turning ch.

Row 10: Repeat Row 8.

NOTE Row 11 starts the alternate blocks for the next basketweave.

Row 11: Ch 2, turn. Sk st at base of chs. Fpdc around each of next 4 sts, bpdc around each of next 4 sts, fpdc around each of next 4 sts. Hdc into top of turning ch.

Row 12: Ch 2, turn. Sk st at base of chs. Bpdc around each of next 4 sts, fpdc around each of next 4 sts, bpdc around each of next 4 sts. Hdc into top of turning ch.

Rows 13–14: Repeat Rows 5–6.

Rows 15–134: Repeat Rows 7–14 fifteen times.

Row 135: Ch 1, turn. Sc into each st across, ending with sc in top of turning ch. Total 14 sc.

Row 136 (starts edging): Ch 1, turn. Sc into each st across to last st. Sc 2 in last st, then continue to sc evenly down the long side of scarf (1 sc at the end of every row). Work 2 sc in bottom corner. *Ch 15 to start fringe. Sl st in second ch from hook and in each ch up fringe. Total 14 sl sts. Sc at base of fringe and in each of next 4 sts along scarf bottom. Repeat from * twice. Ch 15 to start final fringe. Sl st in second ch from hook and in each chain up fringe. Total 14 sl sts. Work 2 sc into corner where current fringe started.

Sc evenly up side of scarf. Work fringe as at other end, ending with sc at base of last fringe. Fo.

Finishing

With tapestry needle, weave in ends. Lightly steam block scarf.

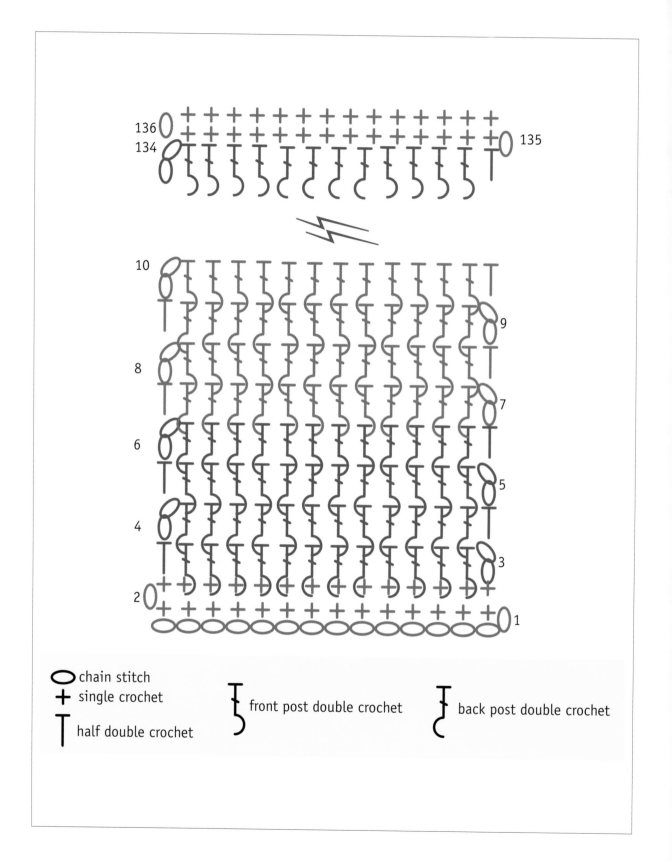

O chain stitch
+ single crochet
T half double crochet
ʒ front post double crochet
ʒ back post double crochet

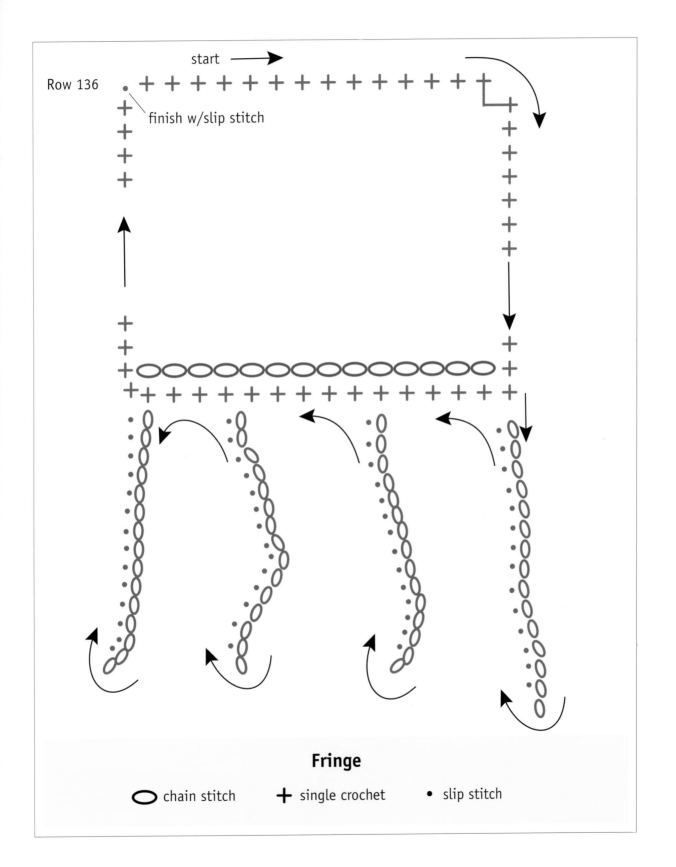

Fringe

⬭ chain stitch + single crochet • slip stitch

Curly Sunflowers

Florafil has a festive texture and color palette. I chose a simple shell pattern to let the yarn do the talking. A nice thick fringe shows off the squiggles.

This product is manufactured right down the road from me in Kennett Square, Pennsylvania. It's appropriate that the colorway, Helenium "Mardi Gras," is from Florafil's American Wildflowers Collection, since Kennett Square is also the home of Longwood Gardens—the country's top horticultural showplace.

MEASUREMENTS

66 inches (167.6 centimeters) by 6 inches (15.2 centimeters), plus 8 inches (20.3 centimeters) of fringe at each end

MATERIALS

Florafil Super Soft Cotton Yarn, 97% cotton, 3% nylon, 3.5 ounces/100 grams, 125 yards/ 114.3 meters

Bulky

Helenium "Mardi Gras," 2 skeins

Crochet hook size K (6.50 mm) or size needed to obtain gauge

Tapestry needle

9-inch (22.9 centimeter) piece of cardboard for making fringe

STITCHES AND ABBREVIATIONS

Chain (ch), chains (chs)

Double crochet (dc)

Fasten off (fo)

Right side (RS)

Single crochet (sc)

Skip (sk)

GAUGE

Gauge is flexible for this project. Suggested gauge is 9 stitches and 5 rows in dc/4 inches (10.2 centimeters), unblocked.

For gauge swatch, ch 15. Final 3 chs count as dc.

Row 1: Dc in fourth ch from hook and in each ch across. Total 13 dc.

NOTE Because of the yarn's texture, it can be hard to see where the stitches are at first. Use your fingers to open the chs so you don't inadvertently put two stitches in one chain or skip a chain by accident. This gets easier after the first row.

Row 2: Ch 3 (counts as dc), turn. Sk st at base of chs. Dc in each st across, working final dc into top of turning ch. Total 13 dc.

Repeat Row 2 until swatch measures at least 4.5 inches (11.4 centimeters).

Scarf

Ch 24.

Row 1 (RS): Sc in 9th ch from hook. *Ch 2, sk 2 ch, dc in next ch. Ch 2, sk 2 ch, sc in next ch. Repeat from * once. Ch 2, sk 2 ch, dc in final ch.

Row 2: Ch 1, turn. Sc at base of ch (in dc from previous row). *Work 5 dc in next sc (shell made), sc in next dc. Repeat from * once. Work 5 dc in next sc, sk 2 ch, sc in next ch.

Row 3: Ch 5, turn. *Sc in third dc of 5 in shell, ch 2, dc in next sc, ch 2. Repeat from * once. Sc in third dc of next shell, ch 2, dc in next sc.

Repeat Rows 2 and 3 until scarf is 66 inches (167.6 centimeters) long. Fo.

Fringe

There are six sets of fringe on each end, evenly spaced. Each set has four long strands folded over to make eight strands.

Loosely wrap yarn around cardboard 48 times, starting and ending at the bottom. (You can do this in two batches if it is easier for you.) Cut the bottom of the yarn.

Take four strands and line them up so the ends match. Fold in half.

With RS of the scarf facing you, poke your crochet hook through from back to front. Pull the folded part of one fringe bundle through to the back. Pull the loose ends through the fold, then pull taut. Repeat evenly across so there are six groups of fringe. Repeat on other end.

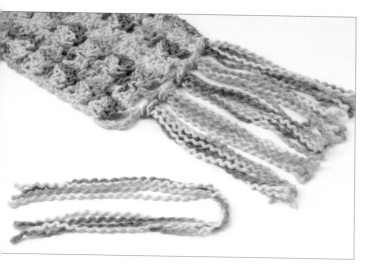

Repeat rows 2 and 3

O chain stitch **+** single crochet **T** double crochet

Holiday Dazzle

SKILL LEVEL

▬▬▬▭
INTERMEDIATE

Add some sparkle to a special occasion with this chic little shaped scarf worked from the top down in an updated chevron pattern.

MEASUREMENTS

63 inches (160 centimeters) by 7 inches (17.8 centimeters) at widest point

MATERIALS

Plymouth Holiday Lights, 72% acrylic, 25% wool, 3% polyester, 209 yards/191 meters, 3.53 ounces/ 100 grams

4

Medium

Black (8217), 1 skein

Crochet hook size K (6.5 mm) or size needed to obtain gauge

Tapestry needle

STITCHES AND ABBREVIATIONS

Chain (ch), chains (chs)

Double crochet (dc)

Double crochet 2 together (dc2tog)

Double treble drochet (dtr)

Fasten off (fo)

Half double crochet (hdc)

Loop (lp), loops (lps)

Right side (RS)

Single crochet (sc)

Skip (sk)

Slip stitch (sl st)

Stitch (st), stitches (sts)

Treble crochet (tr)

Wrong side (WS)

Yarn over (yo)

GAUGE

11 stitches and 6 rows in dc/4 inches (10.2 centimeters), unblocked

For gauge swatch, ch 20. Last 3 chs count as first dc on next row.

Row 1: Dc in fourth ch from hook and in each ch across. Total 18 dc.

Row 2: Ch 3 (counts as dc), turn. Sk st at base of chs. Dc in each dc across, ending with dc in top of turning ch. Total 18 dc.

Repeat Row 2 until swatch measures 4.5 inches (11.4 centimeters).

Special Stitches

Double Crochet Two Together (dc2tog)

This joins two double crochet stitches into one. Yo, insert hook in next st, yo, pull up lp (3 lps on hook), yo, pull through 2 lps (2 lps on hook). Do not complete the stitch. 2 lps remain on hook.

Yo, insert hook in next st, yo, pull up lp (4 lps on hook), yo, pull through 2 lps (3 lps on hook), yo, pull through all 3 lps.

Double Treble Crochet (dtr)

Yo three times, insert hook where indicated, yo, pull up lp (5 lps on hook), [yo, pull through 2 lps] four times.

Scarf

Ch 152. Last 3 chs count as first dc on next row.

Row 1 (RS): Dc in third ch from hook. *Dc in each of next 2 chs, [dc2tog over next 2 chs] twice, dc in each of next 2 chs, [2 dc in next ch] twice. Repeat from * until 9 chs remain. Dc in each of next 2 chs, [dc2tog over next 2 chs] twice, dc in each of next 2 chs, 2 dc in next ch.

> **NOTE** At the bottom of each chevron, remember to work dc2tog *twice*. You will be making four stitches into two. At the top of the chevron, work 2 dc in *each* of the top two stitches. You will be making two stitches into four.

Row 2 (WS): Ch 1, turn. Sl st in each of first 11 sts. The final sl st is at the top of a chevron, in the inner pair of dc. Ch 3 (counts as dc), dc into dc at base of chs. *Dc in each of next 2 dc, [dc2tog over next 2 dc] twice, dc in each of next 2 dc, [2 dc in next dc] twice. Repeat from * until 19 dc remain. Dc in each of next 2 dc, [dc2tog over next 2 dc] twice, dc in each of next 2 dc, 2 dc in next dc. Leave remaining sts unworked. Your row should be symmetrical.

Rows 3–7: Repeat Row 2.

Row 8: Ch 1, turn. Sl st in each of first 10 dc. Sc in next dc, hdc in next dc, dc in next dc, tr in next dc, dtr in each of next 2 dc, tr in next dc, hdc in next dc, sc in next dc, sl st in next dc. Leave remaining sts unworked. Fo.

Finishing

With tapestry needle, weave in ends.

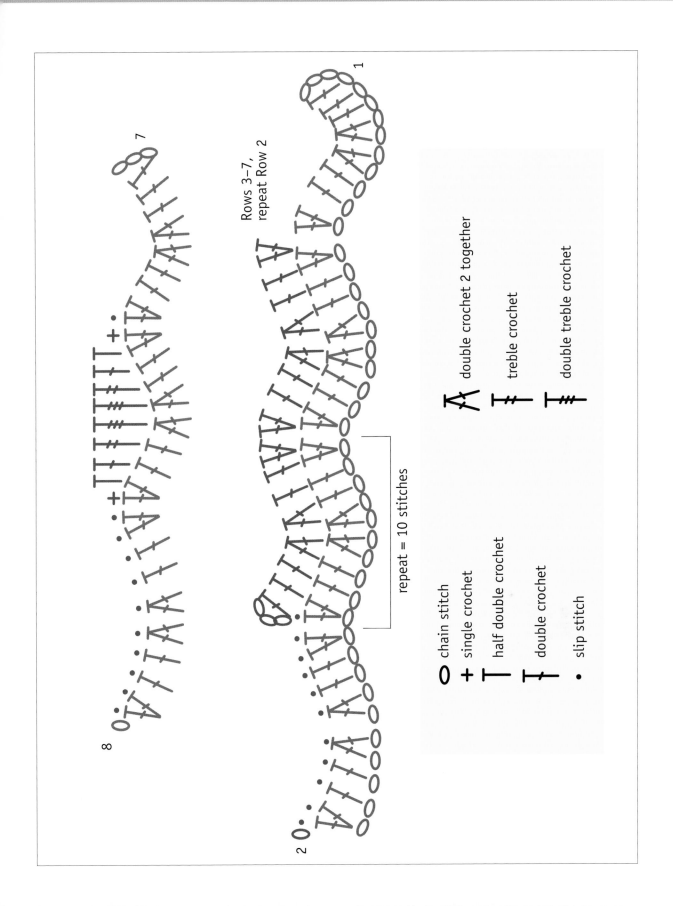

Rows 3–7,
repeat Row 2

repeat = 10 stitches

double crochet 2 together

treble crochet

double treble crochet

chain stitch

single crochet

half double crochet

double crochet

slip stitch

Swallowtail Cowl

This soft, scrunchy cowl in Estelle yarn, a blend of superwash merino, cashmere, and nylon from SpaceCadet Creations, uses Tunisian honeycomb stitch to showcase the variegations in the yarn. It is worked flat, then seamed. A slit down the back allows the cowl to float gracefully over the shoulders.

MEASUREMENTS

Circumference around neck, 19 inches (48.3 centimeters); circumference at shoulders, 25 inches (63.5 centimeters); length, 10 inches (25.4 centimeters)

NOTE To make a cowl with a wider neck, simply increase your starting chain by six chains for every inch you want to add to the neck circumference. Stop decreasing after Row 12.

MATERIALS

SpaceCadet Creations Estelle, 80% superwash merino wool, 10% cashmere, 10% nylon, 3.5 ounces/100 grams, 430 yards/393.2 meters

Super Fine

Old Cottage Bricks (110624-006), 1 skein

Tunisian crochet hook size K (6.5 mm) or size needed to obtain gauge

Crochet hook size J (6.0 mm) or one size smaller than Tunisian hook

Tapestry needle

STITCHES AND ABBREVIATIONS

Chain (ch), chains (chs)

Fasten off (fo)

Loop (lp), loops (lps)

Right side (RS)

Single crochet (sc)

Skip (sk)

Slip stitch (sl st)

Tunisian purl stitch (Tps)

Tunisian simple stitch (Tss)

Wrong side (WS)

Yarn over (yo)

GAUGE

22 stitches and 14 rows in Tunisian honeycomb stitch/4 inches (10.2 centimeters), blocked

For gauge swatch, ch 25.

Row 1 forward: Tps in second ch from hook. *Tss in next ch, Tps in next ch. Repeat from * across.

Row 1 return: Yo, pull through 1 lp. *Yo, pull through 2 lps. Repeat from * until 1 lp remains on hook.

NOTE Work every return pass on the gauge swatch this way.

Row 2: Sk first vertical bar. *Tss in next Tps, Tps in next Tss. Repeat from * across until 2 sts remain. Tss in next st. Tss in final st, inserting hook behind vertical bar and the horizontal thread behind it for stability.

Row 3: Sk first vertical bar. *Tps in next Tss, Tss in next Tps. Repeat from * across. Return.

Repeat Rows 2–3 until swatch measures 4.5 inches (11.4 centimeters).

Special Stitches

Tunisian Honeycomb

Row 1 forward: Sk first vertical bar. *Tps in next vertical bar, Tss in next vertical bar. Repeat from * across, ending with Tss.

Row 1 return: Yo, pull through 1 lp. *Yo, pull through 2 lps. Repeat from * until 1 lp remains on hook.

Row 2 forward: Sk first vertical bar. *Tss in next st, Tps in next st. (The stitches are staggered: Work a Tss into the Tps from the previous row, and a Tps into the Tss from the previous row. This creates the honeycomb.) Repeat from * across, ending with Tss.

NOTE The last stitch is always a Tss. Work it into the final vertical bar and the horizontal thread that runs behind it for stability.

Row 2 return: As Row 1 return.

Repeat Rows 1 and 2 for honeycomb pattern.

Cowl

NOTE Each row decreases one stitch on each end from Row 2 through Row 12. This is done with a slip stitch at the beginning of a forward pass, and a yarn over, pull through 2 at the beginning of the return pass. Starting with Row 13, the neck is worked straight up with no decreases.

Ch 117.

Row 1 forward (RS): Tps in second ch from hook, *Tss in next ch, Tps in next ch. Repeat from * across, ending with Tss in last ch. Do not turn.

Row 1 return: Yo, pull through 1 lp. *Yo, pull through 2 lps. Repeat from * until l lp remains on hook.

Row 2 forward: Sk first vertical bar. Insert hook in Tps, yo, pull through both lps. Sl st made. (This makes a decrease at the beginning of the forward pass.) *Tps in Tss, Tss in Tps. Repeat from * across, working Tss in final st. Total 116 lps on hook.

Row 2 return: *Yo, pull through 2 lps. (This makes a decrease at the beginning of the return pass.) Repeat from * across until 1 lp remains on hook.

Row 3 forward: As Row 2 forward. (The final Tss will be placed into the slanted st at the end of Row 2; it is slanted because of the decrease at the beginning of the return pass on Row 2.) Total 114 lps on hook.

Row 3 return: As Row 2 return.

Rows 4–12: As Row 3 forward and return. Each forward pass will have 2 fewer stitches than the previous row's forward pass. Total 96 sts on the forward pass of Row 12.

NOTE The decreases are complete when the return pass of Row 12 is done. From now on, do not slip stitch at the beginning of the forward pass.

Work each return as follows: Yo, pull through 1 lp. *Yo, pull through 2 lps. Repeat from * until 1 lp remains on hook.

Row 13: Sk first vertical bar. *Tss in Tps, Tps in Tss. Repeat from * across, working Tss in final st. Return.

Row 14: Sk first vertical bar. *Tps in Tss, Tss in Tps. Repeat from * across, working Tss in final st. Return.

Repeat Rows 13 and 14 until cowl measures 9.5 inches (24.1 centimeters), ending with Row 14.

Final Row and Border: Change to regular crochet hook, one size smaller than Tunisian hook. Sk first vertical bar. *Insert hook in next st as for Tss, yo, pull up lp, yo, pull through 2 lps (sc made). Insert hook in next st as for Tps, yo, pull up lp, yo, pull through 2 lps (sc made). Repeat from * across. Sc evenly down side, across bottom, and up other side, working 2–3 sc in bottom corners to keep flat. Join to first st with sl st. Fo.

Finishing

With tapestry needle, weave in ends. Lightly steam block on WS if desired.

Seam

Rows 1–12 are left unseamed to create the swallowtail.

Put RS together so WS is facing you. For right-handers, arrange the folded piece so bottom of the cowl is on the left and the swallowtail is in the upper left; for left-handers, arrange the folded piece so the bottom of the cowl is on the right with the swallowtail in the upper right.

Join yarn through both thicknesses at top of cowl. *Insert hook through the top of the sc sts on both pieces and work a sl st. Continue in each set of sc until you reach the beginning of the swallowtail. Fo.

With tapestry needle, weave in ends. Lightly steam block seam if desired. Turn RS out.

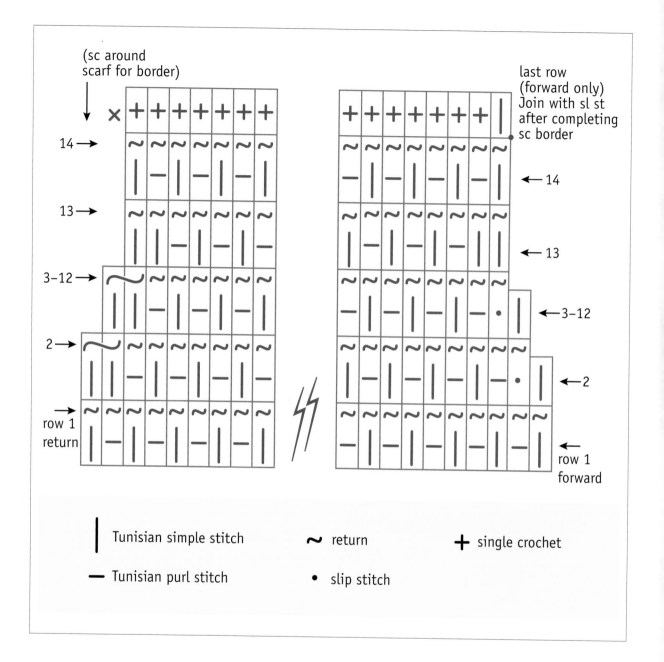

(sc around scarf for border)

last row (forward only) Join with sl st after completing sc border

14 →

13 →

3–12 →

2 →

row 1 return

← 14

← 13

←3–12

←2

row 1 forward

| Tunisian simple stitch

~ return

+ single crochet

— Tunisian purl stitch

• slip stitch

Electric Lime

Talk about cozy! Super bulky Bazinga thick-and-thin yarn is worked in Tunisian net stitch—also called Tunisian full stitch—to create an eye-catching, wonderfully warm scarf.

99

MEASUREMENTS

66 inches (167.6 centimeters) by 6 inches (15.2 centimeters)

MATERIALS

Plymouth Bazinga, 53% wool, 47% acrylic, 1.76 ounces/50 grams, 55 yards/50 meters

6

Super Bulky

01, Purples and Greens, 5 balls

Tunisian crochet hook size N (10 mm) or size needed to obtain gauge

Crochet hook size N (10 mm) or size that corresponds to Tunisian hook (optional)

Tapestry needle or size H (5.00 mm) crochet hook for weaving in ends

STITCHES AND ABBREVIATIONS

Chain (ch), chains (chs)

Fasten off (fo)

Loop (lp), loops (lps)

Right side (RS)

Single crochet (sc)

Skip (sk)

Slip stitch (sl st)

Space (sp), spaces (sps)

Tunisian net stitch (Tns)

Tunisian simple stitch (Tss)

Wrong side (WS)

Yarn over (yo)

GAUGE

Gauge is flexible for this project. Suggested gauge is 10 sts and 8 rows in Tns/4 inches (10.2 centimeters), unblocked.

NOTE The rows are staggered. When testing gauge, be sure to count every row, not every other row.

For gauge swatch, work in pattern through Row 10.

NOTE If your gauge is correct, you can use your swatch as the beginning of the scarf.

Special Stitches

Tunisian Net Stitch (Tns), Also Known as Tunisian Full Stitch

This stitch pattern is defined by the way the stitches are placed. Each stitch is made by putting the hook from the front of the work to the back in the space between the stitches. Tunisian knit stitches go from front to back *within* a stitch. That is the only difference. The net pattern is created by staggering the stitches.

Ch 12.

Row 1 forward: Insert hook in second ch from hook. Yo, pull up lp. *Insert hook in next ch, yo, pull up lp. Repeat from * across. Total 12 lps on hook.

Row 1 return: Yo, pull through 1 lp. *Yo, pull through 2 lps. Repeat from * until 1 lp remains on hook.

NOTE Work every return pass this way.

Row 2: Sk first 2 vertical bars. Tns into space between *second* and *third* sts, poking hook from front to back. Tns into each sp to final vertical bar. Tss into final vertical bar and the horizontal thread behind it for stability. Total 12 lps on hook. Return.

NOTE The photo above shows the spaces between the vertical bars. You will be working into those spaces, not into the stitches.

Row 3: Sk first vertical bar. Tns into sp between *first* and *second* vertical bars. Tns into each sp to last sp. Sk that last sp. Tss into final vertical bar and horizontal thread behind it for stability. Total 12 lps on hook. Return.

Repeat Rows 1 and 2 for pattern.

> **NOTE** To keep the same number of loops on the hook while creating the staggered net pattern, skip the first space at the beginning of one row and do not skip any spaces at the far end of that row. You may have to look closely to find that last space. On the next row, work into the first space but skip the last space at the far end. Count your stitches to make sure you have the correct number. For this pattern, you should have 12 loops on the hook at the end of every forward pass.

Scarf

Ch 12.

Row 1 forward: Insert hook in second ch from hook. Yo, pull up lp. *Insert hook in next ch, yo, pull up lp. Repeat from * across. Total 12 lps on hook.

Row 1 return: Yo, pull through 1 lp. *Yo, pull through 2 lps. Repeat from * until 1 lp remains on hook.

> **NOTE** Work every return pass this way.

Row 2: Sk first 2 vertical bars. Tns into space between *second* and *third* sts, poking hook from front to back. Tns into each sp to final vertical bar. Tss into final vertical bar and the horizontal thread behind it for stability. Total 12 lps on hook. Return.

Row 3: Sk first vertical bar. Tns into sp between *first* and *second* vertical bars. Tns into each sp to last sp. Sk that last sp. Tss into final vertical bar and horizontal thread behind it for stability. Total 12 lps on hook. Return.

Repeat Rows 2 and 3 until scarf measures 65 inches (165.1 centimeters).

> **NOTE** Switch to regular crochet hook for the final row if desired.

Final row, beginning of border: Insert hook in first sp as for Tns, yo, pull up lp, yo, pull through 2 lps (sc made). Continue to work a sc in each sp across, working 2 or 3 sc in the corner to keep it flat. Sc evenly down the side, across the bottom, and up the other side, working 2 or 3 sc in each corner. When you get back to the beginning, join to first st with sl st. Fo.

Finishing

With tapestry needle or size H (5.0 mm) crochet hook, weave in ends. Lightly steam block on WS if desired.

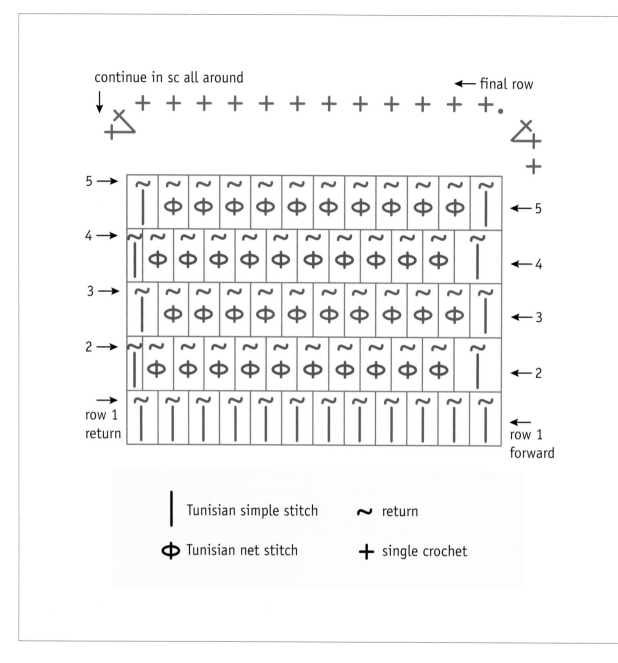

continue in sc all around

← final row

5 →

← 5

4 →

← 4

3 →

← 3

2 →

← 2

→
row 1
return

←
row 1
forward

| Tunisian simple stitch   ~ return

Φ Tunisian net stitch   + single crochet

Monet's Village

SKILL LEVEL

■■■□
INTERMEDIATE

The technique known as filet crochet combines open and filled squares in a mesh pattern that is often used for delicate place-mats and tablecloths. Geometric patterns, flowers, butterflies— almost anything can be represented pictorially in filet crochet by arranging the open and closed blocks appropriately.

I decided on a scalloped look for this scarf to give it more motion and interest than a rectangular pattern, and to show off the impressionistic hues in the yarn. The scarf is finished with a two rows of single crochet down the long straight side.

MEASUREMENTS

56 inches (142.2 centimeters) by 6 inches (15.2 centimeters)

MATERIALS

Jojoland Melody Superwash, 100% wool, 1.76 ounces/50 grams, 220 yards/200 meters

Super Fine

MS08, purple and green: 1 skein

Crochet hook size E (3.5 mm) or size needed to obtain gauge

Crochet hook size D (3.25) or one size smaller than hook used for body of scarf

Tapestry needle

STITCHES AND ABBREVIATIONS

Chain stitch (ch)

Double crochet (dc)

Fasten off (fo)

Right side (RS)

Single crochet (sc)

Skip (sk)

Wrong side (WS)

GAUGE

Gauge is flexible for this project. Suggested gauge is 26 stitches and 8 rows in dc/4 inches (10.1 centimeters) blocked.

For gauge swatch, ch 32. Last 3 chs count as dc on Row 1.

Row 1: Dc in fourth ch from hook and in each ch across. Total 30 dc.

Row 2: Ch 3 (counts as dc), turn. Sk st at base of chs. Dc in each dc across. Total 30 dc.

Repeat Row 2 until swatch measures 4.5 inches (11.4 centimeters).

NOTES At the beginning of a row that starts with open blocks, ch 5 (counts as dc and ch-2).

When working the final stitch on a row into an open block below, dc into third of the 5 chs.

When working a solid block into an open block, work center 2 dc into the chain space, not into the chain stitches.

Special Stitch

Filet Crochet

Filet crochet is a grid of solid and open squares made in double crochet and chain stitches. In this scarf pattern, each square consists of four stitches, either dc, ch, ch, dc, or 4 dc.

When two solid blocks are adjacent, they share the middle stitch (the wall between the blocks), making 7 stitches total. Using the same formula, a row of six solid blocks has 19 stitches total.

Filet instructions are not given word-for-word in text. Instead, a chart of solid and open blocks is presented on page 106. Read the chart from bottom to top. Right-side rows go from right to left; wrong-side rows from left to right. Open squares correspond to open spaces; solid squares indicate a solid block of dc.

In this pattern, increases are made in sets of two blocks. To increase two blocks, ch 8 (last 3 chs count as first dc on next row), dc into fourth ch from hook and in each of next 4 chs, then dc in dc on the end of the previous row.

To decrease, simply leave stitches unworked.

Scarf

Chain 21. Last 3 chs count as first dc on Row 1.

Start at bottom right of chart. Follow the chart from right to left on RS rows and from left to right on WS rows. Turn your work at the beginning of every row.

NOTE As you move up the chart, you can cover the completed rows in the diagram with a sticky note so you can clearly see which row you are on.

The photographs show the work at the end of Row 4 and the increase at the beginning of Row 5. Note that the seventh stitch on Row 5 is directly above the farthest right stitch from Row 4.

When you reach the end of the chart, do not fo.

Trim

Switch to smaller hook.

Row 1: Sc evenly down straight side of scarf.

Row 2: Ch 1, turn. Sc in each sc up straight side of scarf. Fo.

Finishing

With tapestry needle, weave in ends. Lightly steam block on WS if desired.

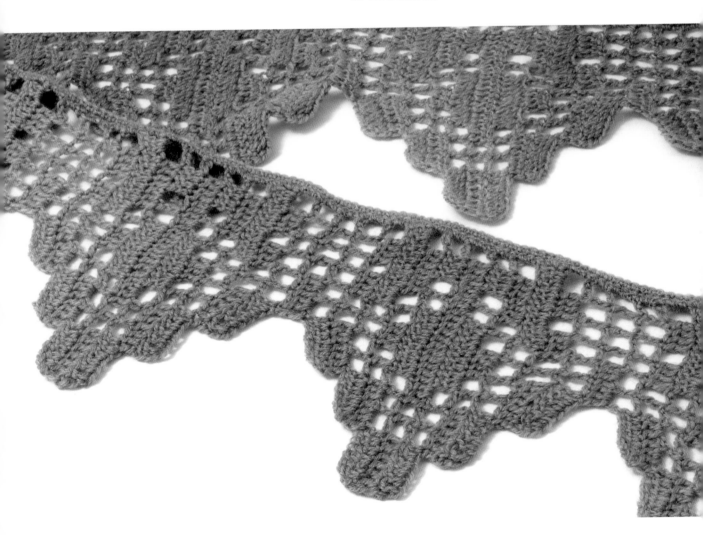

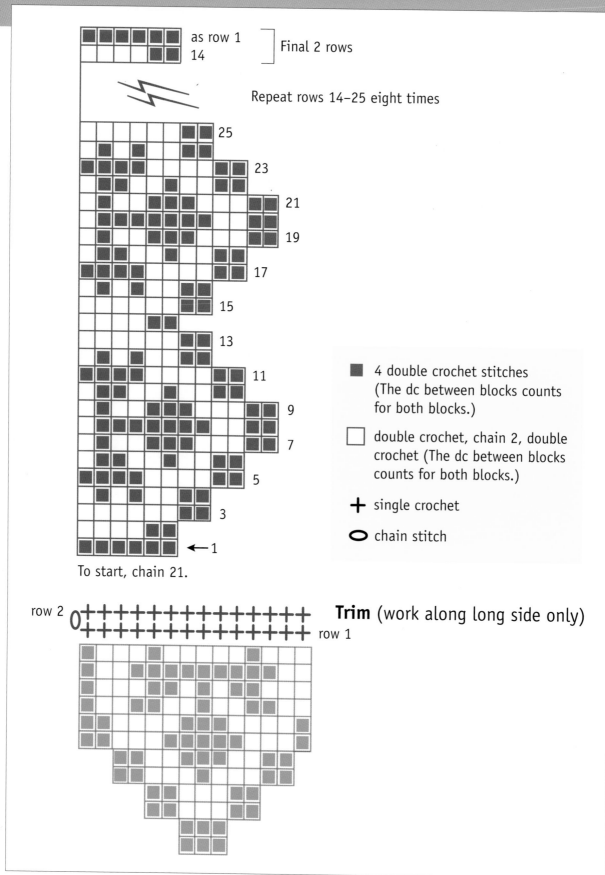

as row 1

14

Final 2 rows

Repeat rows 14–25 eight times

25

23

21

19

17

15

13

11

9

7

5

3

■ 4 double crochet stitches
(The dc between blocks counts
for both blocks.)

☐ double crochet, chain 2, double
crochet (The dc between blocks
counts for both blocks.)

+ single crochet

O chain stitch

← 1

To start, chain 21.

row 2 O

Trim (work along long side only)

row 1

Ridged Collar

SKILL LEVEL

■■■◻
INTERMEDIATE

This pattern takes advantage of the natural ridges created by Tunisian knit and purl stitches. After the body of the scarf is created, a decrease row cinches the scarf. Black edging gives the collar a formal finish; the scallop shapes soften the straight white lines. Hold the scarf closed with a decorative pin (like this one from DesignsByRomi.com) so you can adjust it to fit under or over whatever coat or jacket you are wearing.

MEASUREMENTS

Diameter of inner circle 6.5 inches (16.5 centimeters), diameter of outer circle 16 inches (40.6 centimeters), width 5 inches (12.7 centimeters)

MATERIALS

Louet Gems, 100% merino wool, 3.5 ounces/100 grams, 225 yards/205 meters

Fine

Color A: Pure White (80-2703-2), 1 skein

Color B: Black (80-2222-33), 1 skein

Tunisian crochet hook size H (5.0 mm) or size needed to obtain gauge

Crochet hook size H (5.0 mm) or size that corresponds to Tunisian hook

Tapestry needle

STITCHES AND ABBREVIATIONS

Chain (ch), chains (chs)

Fasten off (fo)

Loop (lp), loops (lps)

Right side (RS)

Single crochet (sc)

Skip (sk)

Slip stitch (sl st)

Tunisian knit stitch (Tks)

Tunisian purl stitch (Tps)

Tunisian simple stitch (Tss)

Wrong side (WS)

Yarn over (yo)

GAUGE

23 stitches and 18 rows in pattern/4 inches (10.2 cm), blocked

For gauge swatch, ch 29.

Row 1 forward: Tps in second ch from hook. Tps into each of next 2 chs. *Tss in each of next 3 chs, Tps in each of next 3 chs. Repeat from * across. Tss in final ch. Total 29 lps on hook. Do not turn.

Row 1 return: Yo, pull through 1 lp. *Yo, pull through 2 lps. Repeat from * until 1 lp remains on hook.

NOTE Work every return pass this way.

Row 2: Sk first vertical bar. Tps in each of next 3 Tps. *Tks in each of next 3 Tks, Tps in each of next 3 Tps. Repeat from * across. Tss in final st. Return.

NOTE Work the final Tss into the vertical bar and the horizontal thread that runs behind it for stability.

Rows 3–20: Repeat Row 2. Fo. Gently steam block your swatch on WS, then check your gauge.

Scarf

NOTE Each forward pass has one unworked vertical bar at the beginning, then alternates 3 Tps with 3 Tks, ending with 3 Tps and one Tss. On the first row, Tks and Tss are essentially the same, since there are no vertical bars yet—each stitch is worked into a chain. For Tps on that row, bring the yarn to the front as you would for any Tps, working into the chain.

With A, ch 239.

Row 1 (RS) forward: Tps in second ch from hook and in each of next 2 chs, *Tks in each of next 3 chs, Tps in each of next 3 chs. Repeat from * across. Tss into final st. Return.

Row 1 return: Yo, pull through 1 lp. *Yo, pull through 2 lps. Repeat from * until 1 lp remains on hook.

NOTE Work all return passes this way.

Row 2: Sk first vertical bar. Tps in each of next 3 Tps, *Tks in each of next 3 Tks, Tps in each of next 3 Tps. Repeat from * across. Tss in final st. Return.

Rows 3–14: Repeat Row 2.

Row 15 (decrease row): Sk first vertical bar. *Insert hook into next 3 sts, keeping hook to front of work. Yo, pull up lp. Insert hook into next 2 sts, yo, pull up lp Repeat from * until 3 sts remain. Insert hook into next 2 sts, yo, pull up lp. Tss in final st. Total 97 lps on hook. Return.

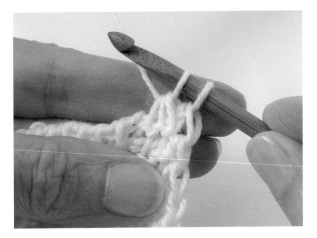

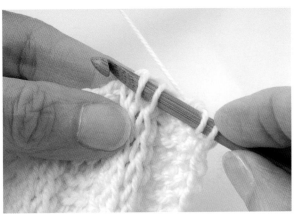

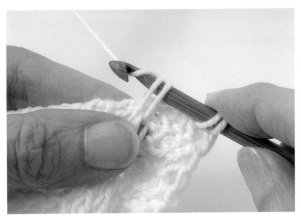

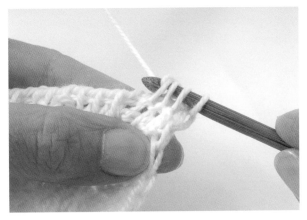

Trim

> **NOTE** You can use your Tunisian hook as a regular crochet hook, or switch to a regular hook.

With WS facing, join B in a corner of beginning chain. Ch 1. Sc in each of next 3 sts. *Ch 5, sk 3 sts, sc in each of next 3 sts. Repeat from * across until 1 st remains. Sc in final st. (You will have 4 sc at the end of this row.) Total 39 ch lps.

Row 16 (finishing row). Sk first vertical bar. Insert hook in next st as for Tss. Yo, pull up lp, yo, pull through both lps (sc made). Continue in sc across. Fo.

Row 2: Ch 1, turn. Sc in third of the 4 sc. *Dc 7 in ch arch, sc in second of next group of 3 sc. Repeat from * across. Sc into ch 1 from Row 1 of trim. Fo.

Finishing

With tapestry needle, weave in ends. Lightly steam block if desired.

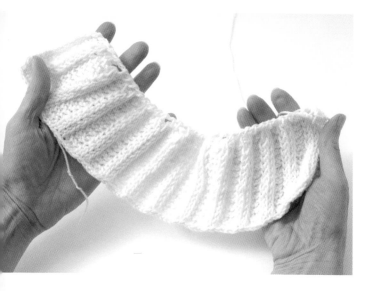

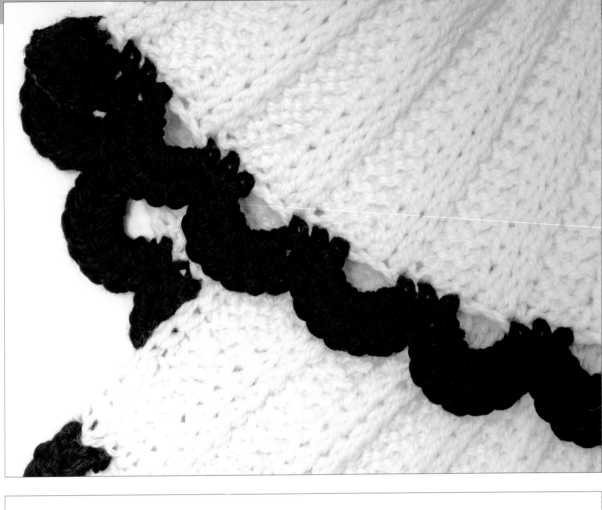

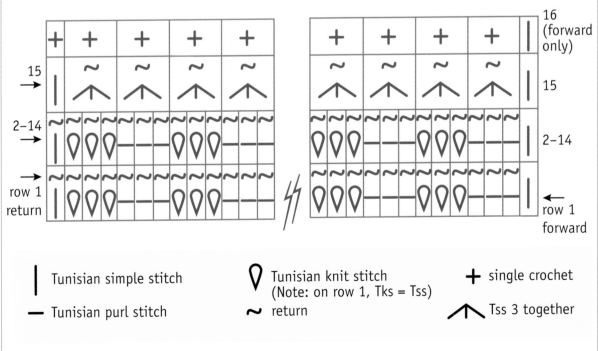

	Tunisian simple stitch	⋃	Tunisian knit stitch (Note: on row 1, Tks = Tss)	+	single crochet
—	Tunisian purl stitch	~	return	∧	Tss 3 together

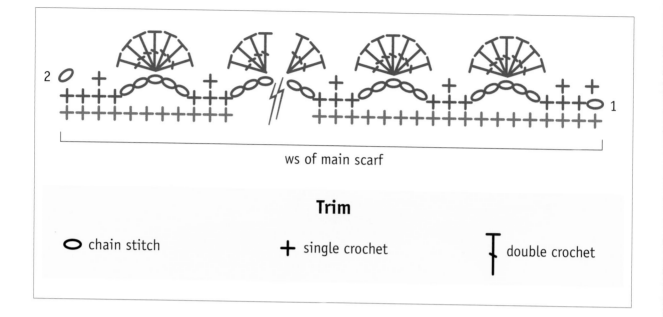

ws of main scarf

Trim

⭘ chain stitch   ✛ single crochet   ⊤ double crochet

Sea Splash

SKILL LEVEL

◼◼◼◻

EXPERIENCED

The variegated greens of this yarn and the curves of the pattern remind me of ocean waves. Chain loops on the edges are the salt spray.

After the first set of waves is crocheted, work the second part of the pattern into the foundation chain to make the scarf symmetrical.

MEASUREMENTS

78 inches (198.1 centimeters) by 5.5 inches (14 centimeters)

MATERIALS

Valley Yarns 2/14, 80% alpaca, 20% silk, 4 oz/113.4 grams; 865 yards/791 meters (sold at Webs Yarn, www.yarn.com, under the Kangaroo Dyer label)

0

Lace

Atlantis, 1 skein

Crochet hook size H (5.00 mm) or size needed to obtain gauge

Tapestry needle

Non-rusting pins for wet-blocking

STITCHES AND ABBREVIATIONS

Chain (ch), chains (chs)

Chain space (ch-sp)

Double crochet (dc)

Fasten off (fo)

Half double crochet (hdc)

Loop (lp), loops (lps)

Right side (RS)

Single crochet (sc)

Skip (sk)

Space (sp), spaces (sps)h

Stitch (st), stitches (sts)

Wrong side (WS)

GAUGE

Gauge is flexible for this project. Suggested gauge with 2 strands held together is 15 stitches and 8 rows in dc/4 inches (10.2 cm), unblocked.

For gauge swatch, *using 2 strands held together,* ch 27. Last 3 chs count as first dc for Row 1.

Row 1: Dc in fourth ch from hook and in each ch across. Total 25 dc.

Row 2: Ch 3 (counts as dc), turn. Sk st at base of chs. Dc in each st across, working final dc in top of turning ch. Total 25 dc.

Rows 3–10: Repeat Row 2.

Special Stitches

Bobble

A 3-dc bobble is made by working each dc until the next-to-last step is completed, then pulling through all loops:

Yo, insert hook where indicated, yo, pull up lp, yo, pull through 2 lps. 2 lps remain on hook. Yo, insert hook in same spot, yo, pull up lp, yo, pull through 2 lps. 3 lps remain on hook. Yo, insert hook in same spot, yo, pull up lp, yo, pull through 2 lps. 4 lps remain on hook. Yo, pull through all 4 lps.

Scarf

Side 1

> **NOTE** The scarf is worked the long way. If you would like your finished scarf to be shorter than the sample, you can subtract a multiple of 17 stitches. Each 17 stitches you subtract will make the scarf approximately 5.5 inches (14 centimeters) shorter.

Foundation: *With 2 strands held together,* ch 258.

Row 1 (RS): Sc in second ch from hook and in each ch across. Total 257 sc.

Row 2 (WS): Ch 1, turn. Sc at base of ch and in each sc across. Total 257 sc.

Row 3 (commence pattern): Ch 1, turn. Sc into each of first 8 sts. *Ch 4, sk 3 sts, sc into each of next 14 sc. Repeat from * to last 11 sts. Ch 4, sk 3 sts, sc into each of last 8 sts.

Row 4: Ch 3 (counts as hdc, ch) turn. Sk sc at base of chs and next sc, sc into each of next 3 sc, ch 1. Into the next ch-4 sp work [dc, ch] 6 times. Sk 3 sc, sc into each of next 3 sc. *Ch 3, sk 2 sc, sc into each of next 3 sc, ch 1. Into next ch-4 sp work [dc, ch] 6 times. Sk 3 sc, sc into each of next 3 sc. Repeat from * to last 2 sc. Ch 1, hdc into last sc.

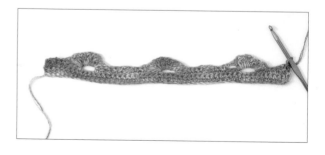

Row 5: Ch 1, turn. Sc into hdc. Ch 2. [Bobble into next ch-sp, ch 2] 7 times. *Sc into next ch-3 sp, ch 2, [Bobble into next ch-sp, ch 2] 7 times. Repeat from * to last ch-3 sp. Sc into last ch-sp.

Row 6: Ch 1, turn. Sc into first sc, 2 sc into first ch-2 sp, sc into top of bobble, 2 sc into next ch-2 sp, [ch 3, 2 sc into next sp] twice, ch 5, [2 sc into next sp, ch 3] twice, 2 sc into next sp, sc into top of next bobble, 2 sc into next sp. *Sk 1 sc, 2 sc into next sp, sc into top of next bobble, 2 sc into next sp, [ch 3, 2 sc into next sp] twice, ch 5, [2 sc into next sp, ch 3] twice, 2 sc into next sp, sc into top of next bobble, 2 sc into next sp. Repeat from * to last sc. Sc in last sc. Fo.

NOTE On this row, each wave has a ch-5 sp at the peak, with two sets of ch-3 spaces on either side.

NOTE The other side of the scarf is worked back into the foundation chain. There are two set-up rows of double crochet, then you will return to the pattern.

Side 2

Row 1: With RS facing, join yarn in first foundation ch. Ch 3 (counts as dc). Dc in each ch across. Total 257 dc.

Row 2: Ch 3 (counts as dc), turn. Dc in each ch across, ending with dc in top of turning chain. Total 257 dc.

Work Rows 3–6 of pattern. Fo.

Finishing

With tapestry needle, weave in ends.

Wet-block your scarf by soaking it in cold water, then gently squeezing out the water in a towel. Pin your scarf into shape with non-rusting pins on a blocking board or thick towels. To get the outermost ch-3 spaces to look distinct, pin them so the spaces are clearly visible. Let dry.

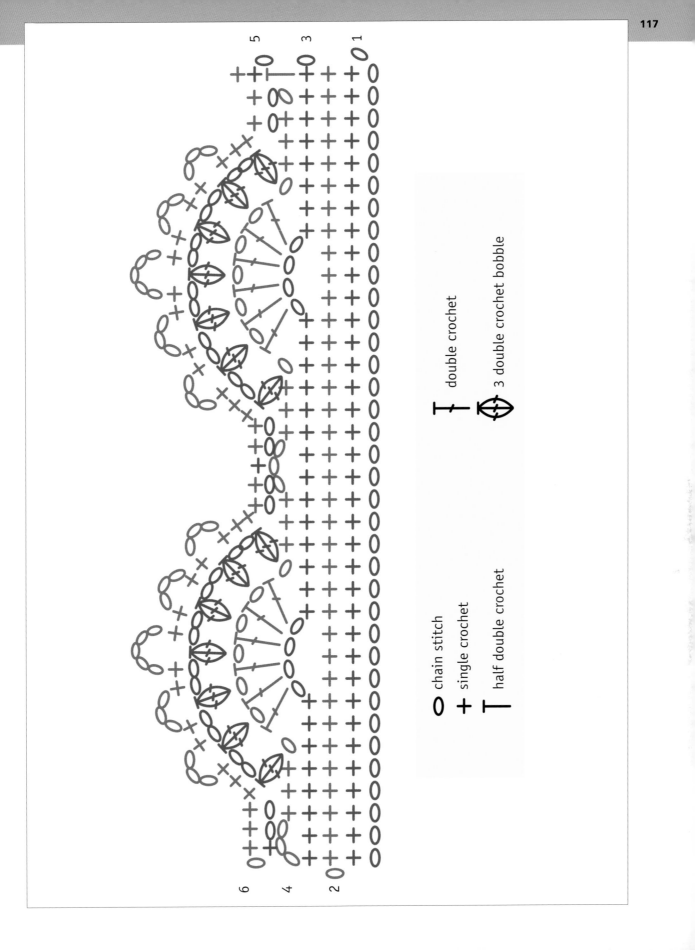

1

3

5

2

4

6

$\mathbf{O}$ chain stitch

$+$ single crochet

$\top$ half double crochet

$\top$ double crochet

3 double crochet bobble

Techniques

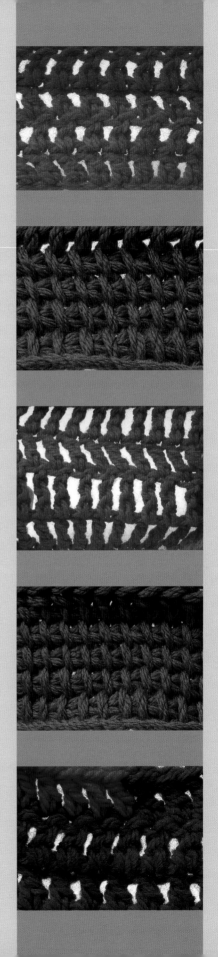

Traditional Crochet

In traditional crochet—the style most people are familiar with—only one stitch at a time is active. Each is worked to completion before the next stitch is begun. Stitch heights progress from the low-profile slip stitch through single crochet, half double crochet, double crochet, treble crochet, and beyond, based on how many times the yarn is wrapped around the hook and how the loops are pulled through other loops. Hooks for traditional crochet are usually 5 to 8 inches long and can be made of metal, plastic, bamboo, wood, or other materials.

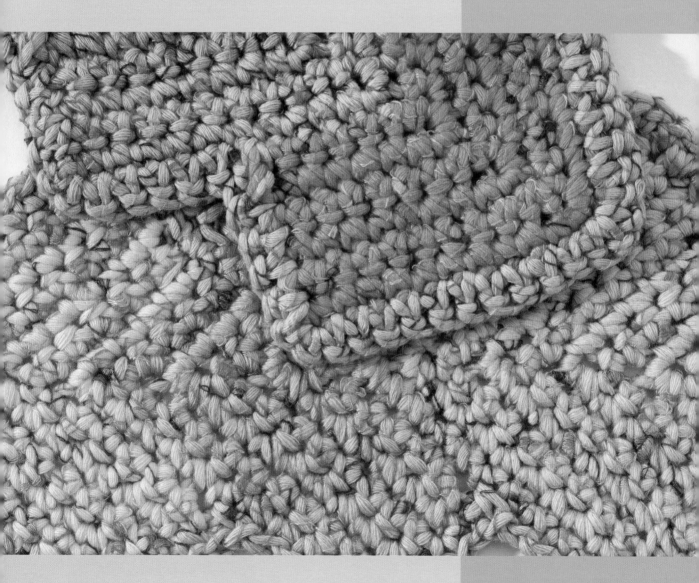

Chain Stitch

1. Attach yarn to hook with slip knot. Yarn over, pull through.

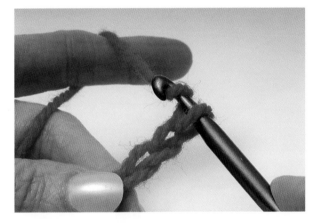

Slip Stitch

1. Insert hook into work where instructed. (This stitch is often used to close a ring.)

2. Yarn over, pull through both loops.

Single Crochet

3. Yarn over, pull through both loops.

1. Insert hook into work where instructed. If you are working into the foundation chain, this will be the second chain from the hook.

2. Yarn over, pull up a loop.

Half Double Crochet

1. Yarn over.

2. Insert hook into work where instructed. If you are working into the foundation chain, this will be the third chain from the hook.

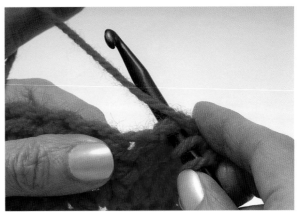

3. Yarn over, pull up a loop.

4. Yarn over, pull through all three loops.

Double Crochet

1. Yarn over.

2. Insert hook into the work where instructed. If you are working into the foundation chain, this will be the fourth chain from the hook.

3. Yarn over, pull up a loop.

5. Yarn over, pull through remaining two loops.

4. Yarn over, pull through two loops.

Treble Crochet

3. Yarn over, pull up a loop.

1. Yarn over twice.

2. Insert hook into the work where instructed. If you are working into the foundation chain, this will be the fifth chain from the hook.

4. Yarn over, pull through two loops.

6. Yarn over, pull through remaining two loops.

5. Yarn over, pull through two loops.

Change Colors or Start a New Yarn

1. Work in pattern as indicated. The photo shows double crochet fabric.

2. Work the next stitch until two loops remain on hook, no matter what type of stitch it is.

4. Continue to work with new yarn.

3. Drop the current yarn to the back. Yarn over with the new color and complete the stitch.

Tunisian Crochet

Tunisian crochet, also known as the "afghan stitch," combines aspects of crocheting and knitting. Like crocheting, it uses a hook and the same hand motions used in traditional crochet; as in knitting, loops are added to the hook so there are many active stitches at once. Tunisian crochet uses either a long hook with a stopper on the end or a shorter hook with a plastic extension to accommodate the many loops that will be on the hook at one time. Tunisian fabric can look knitted, woven, or textured and lacks the "loopy" appearance of traditional crochet.

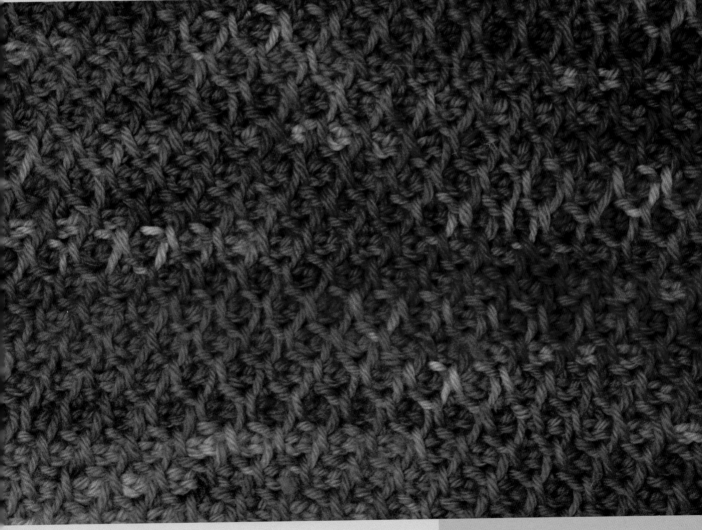

The photo shows a ChiaoGoo bamboo hook with a flexible extension and bead stopper.

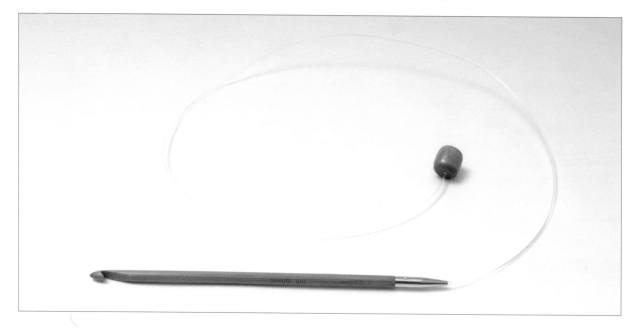

Here is a set of versatile Denise Interchangeable Crochet Hooks.

Different size hooks can be attached to different lengths of plastic cord.

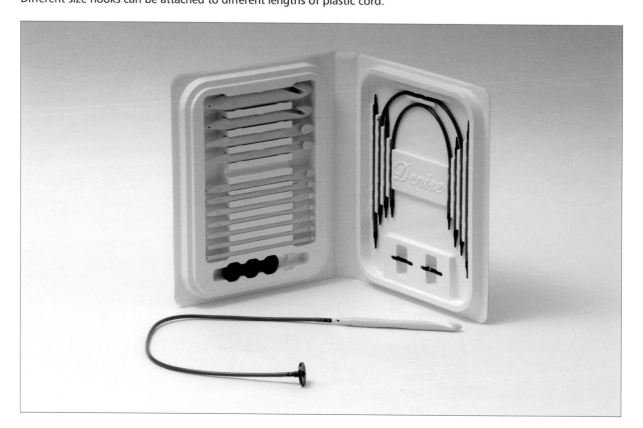

Foundation Row

> **NOTE** All Tunisian fabrics start with this basic row.

Foundation Row Forward

1. Make the number of chain stitches indicated in the pattern.

> **NOTE** The number of Tunisian stitches on subsequent rows will be the same as the number of chains you start with.

2. Insert hook in second chain from hook. Yarn over, pull up loop. There will be two loops on the hook.

> **NOTE** To minimize the curl in Tunisian crochet, you could work into the back bump of the chain.
>
> I usually put the stitches in the regular place, not the back bump, and rely on steam blocking to eliminate the curl.

3. Insert hook in the next chain. Yarn over, pull up loop. Each stitch adds another loop to the hook.

4. Continue in this fashion all the way across.

2. Yarn over, pull through two loops.

5. Count the loops. You should have the same number of loops on the hook as the number of foundation chains.

Foundation Row Return

1. Yarn over, pull through one loop.

3. Repeat Step 2 all the way across until one loop remains on the hook.

> **NOTE** This return method is referred to as the "standard return." Follow this procedure for the return pass unless instructed otherwise.

Tunisian Simple Stitch

Work foundation row forward and return. Look at the finished stitches. You will see a vertical bar for each stitch. These bars are what you will work behind as you make the Tunisian simple stitch forward pass.

2. Put the hook from right to left through the next vertical bar. Keep the hook to the front of the work. Yarn over, pull up a loop. There will be two loops on the hook.

1. Skip the first vertical bar that is on the far right side, directly below the hook.

3. Repeat Step 2 in each stitch across (except for the far left bar), adding a loop to the hook with each stitch.

4. To work the final stitch, identify the final vertical bar and the horizontal thread that runs behind it. Insert the hook so it is behind both of these threads. When viewed from the side, the two threads look like a backwards 6 for right-handers and a regular 6 for lefties.

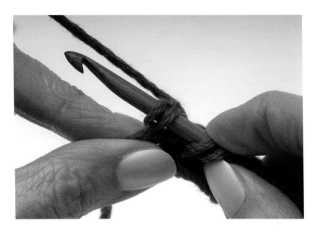

Yarn over, pull up a loop. Count the loops. You should have the same number as you did on the foundation row.

5. Work standard return.

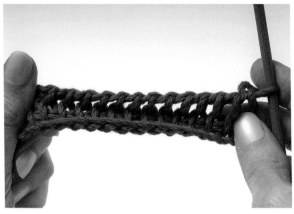

The photo below shows Tunisian simple stitch fabric.

Tunisian Knit Stitch

Work foundation row forward and return. Look at the finished stitches. Each stitch has two "legs" in an upside-down V shape. Instead of keeping the hook to the front like you did in Tunisian simple stitch, for Tunisian knit stitch you will poke the hook from front to back through the center of each stitch.

Forward Pass

1. Skip the first vertical bar that is on the far right side, directly below the hook.
2. Put the hook from front to back through the next stitch. (Stretch the stitch out slightly to see where the two vertical legs are; go right between them, not between two stitches.) Yarn over. Pull up a loop. There will be two loops on the hook.

The photo below shows the hook poking out the back.

3. Repeat Step 2 in each stitch across (except for the far left bar), adding a loop to the hook with each stitch.

4. To work the final stitch, identify the final vertical bar and the horizontal thread that runs behind it. Insert the hook so it is behind both of these threads. When viewed from the side, the two threads look like a backwards 6 for right-handers and a regular 6 for lefties.

NOTE Even though you are working in Tunisian knit stitch, the final stitch is a Tunisian simple stitch. This creates stability along the left side.

Yarn over, pull up a loop. Count the loops. You should have the same number as you did on the foundation row.

5. Work standard return.

The photo shows Tunisian knit stitch fabric.

Here is what it looks like on the back.

Tunisian Purl Stitch

Work foundation row forward and return. Look at the finished stitches. You will see a vertical bar for each stitch. These bars are what you will pick up as you work the Tunisian purl stitch forward pass. Keep the hook to the front of the work, as you did in Tunisian simple stitch.

Forward Pass

1. Skip the first vertical bar that is on the far right side, directly below the hook. Bring the yarn to the front of the hook.

2. Insert the hook into the next vertical bar, keeping the hook to the front of the work. The photo shows the yarn being held in place by my right index finger.

3. Let the yarn go. Bring it toward you in front of the stitch then back under the hook.

4. Yarn over, pull up a loop with that yarn. There will be two loops on the hook.

5. Repeat Step 1 in each stitch across (except for the far left bar), adding a loop to the hook with each stitch. Notice the "purl bump" in the front of each stitch.

6. To work the final stitch, identify the final vertical bar and the horizontal thread that runs behind it.

NOTE You will work a Tunisian simple stitch, not a Tunisian purl stitch, into the final stitch. Do not move the yarn to the front of the hook.

Insert the hook so it is behind both of these threads. When viewed from the side, the two threads look like a backwards 6 for right-handers and a regular 6 for lefties.

Yarn over, pull up a loop. Count the loops. You should have the same number as you did on the foundation row.

7. Work standard return.

The photo shows Tunisian purl fabric.

Change Colors or Start a New Yarn

Sometimes you will need to change colors for a stripe pattern. You will also need to start a new ball of yarn when the previous one runs out. The method is the same in both cases.

The ideal place to start a new yarn is at the end of a return pass.

1. Work return pass until two loops remain on hook. Drop first yarn to the back. Yarn over with new yarn.

Pull through both loops.

Pull old and new tails firmly to hold stitches in place.

2. Continue working with the new yarn, making sure you are using the working end of the yarn and not the short tail.

You can also change colors at the beginning of a return pass. Simply lay the new yarn over the hook, leaving approximately a 3-inch tail, and begin the return pass with the new yarn.

Final Row

The top row of Tunisian crochet looks looser than the previous rows because nothing is worked into it. One way to end the piece neatly is to work single crochet stitches across the top of that row.

1. Insert your hook as you would for whatever stitch pattern you're using. In the example, this is Tunisian simple stitch.

2. Yarn over, pull up loop, yarn over, pull through two loops. This creates a single crochet.

3. Repeat Step 2 across.

Helpful Hints

- Never turn your work. The right side is always facing you.
- Always skip the first vertical bar.
- Pull the yarn snug at the start of each row to keep the edge from getting baggy.
- The final stitch on every forward pass should be a Tunisian simple stitch, regardless of the other stitches on that row.
- Work the final stitch on the forward pass into the vertical bar and the horizontal bar behind it for stability. If you turn that edge toward you, those two threads should look like a backwards 6 for right-handers and a regular 6 for lefties.
- Make sure you count the last stitch of the forward pass and the first stitch of the return pass separately.

- You can work any stitch into any other type of stitch (for example, Tunisian purl stitch into Tunisian knit stitch, or Tunisian simple stitch into Tunisian purl stitch, and so on).
- Count! Check your stitch count regularly to make sure you did not miss picking up a stitch on a forward pass or mistakenly pull through the wrong number of loops on a return pass.
- To reduce the curl in Tunisian crochet, work the foundation row into the back bumps of the starting chains. Working a border around the piece helps, too. To eliminate any remaining curl, gently steam block your finished pieces.

How to Read Crochet Symbol Charts

Crochet instructions can be given in text or charts. A visual representation of a pattern can be very useful in understanding how the item is made.

Here are some guidelines to follow when reading charts for regular crochet:

- First, look at the key to see which symbols represent which stitches. Make sure you know how to make the specified stitches.
- Patterns for crocheting in rows are charted row by row, starting with the foundation chain. Read the pattern starting at bottom left for the chain. Odd-numbered rows will move right to left; even-numbered rows are read left to right. Turn your work at the end of each row unless the chart symbol indicates not to. As you move up, work the new stitches into the stitches they are above in the chart.
- In general, the only time you will actually work into a chain stitch is on Row 1, when you work into the foundation chain. On subsequent rows, if the symbol for the stitch you are supposed to make appears above one or more chains, work that stitch into the chain space rather than the chain stitch itself (unless the pattern or chart specifically says otherwise).
- When part of the pattern is repeated, this will be indicated in the chart to save space.

Here are some guidelines to follow when reading charts for Tunisian crochet:

- First, look at the key to see which symbols represent which stitches. Make sure you know how to make the specified stitches.
- Patterns for Tunisian crochet are charted in pairs of rows, starting after the foundation is complete. The bottom row in each pair represents the forward pass; the top row in each pair indicates the return pass. Read the bottom row right to left; read the top row left to right. This arrangement corresponds to your project, since you do not turn the work in Tunisian crochet.
- When the final part of a Tunisian crochet project is worked in regular crochet stitches, treat that part of the chart as if it were for a regular crochet pattern.
- When part of the pattern is repeated, this will be indicated in the chart to save space.

Resources

STANDARDS & GUIDELINES FOR CROCHET AND KNITTING

Standard Yarn Weight System

Categories of yarn, gauge ranges, and recommended needle and hook sizes

Yarn Weight Symbol & Category Names	0 Lace	1 Super Fine	2 Fine	3 Light	4 Medium	5 Bulky	6 Super Bulky
Type of Yarns in Category	Fingering 10 count crochet thread	Sock, Fingering, Baby	Sport, Baby	DK, Light Worsted	Worsted, Afghan, Aran	Chunky, Craft, Rug	Bulky, Roving
Knit Gauge Range* in Stockinette Stitch to 4 inches	33–40** sts	27–32 sts	23–26 sts	21–24 sts	16–20 sts	12–15 sts	6–11 sts
Recommended Needle in Metric Size Range	1.5–2.25 mm	2.25–3.25 mm	3.25–3.75 mm	3.75–4.5 mm	4.5–5.5 mm	5.5–8 mm	8 mm and larger
Recommended Needle U.S. Size Range	000 to 1	1 to 3	3 to 5	5 to 7	7 to 9	9 to 11	11 and larger
Crochet Gauge* Ranges in Single Crochet to 4 inch	32-42 double crochets**	21–32 sts	16–20 sts	12–17 sts	11–14 sts	8–11 sts	5–9 sts
Recommended Hook in Metric Size Range	Steel*** 1.6–1.4mm Regular hook 2.25 mm	2.25–3.5 mm	3.5–4.5 mm	4.5–5.5 mm	5.5–6.5 mm	6.5–9 mm	9 mm and larger
Recommended Hook U.S. Size Range	Steel*** 6, 7, 8 Regular hook B–1	B–1 to E–4	E–4 to 7	7 to I–9	I–9 to K–10½	K–10½ to M–13	M–13 and larger

* GUIDELINES ONLY: The above reflect the most commonly used gauges and needle or hook sizes for specific yarn categories.

** Lace weight yarns are usually knitted or crocheted on larger needles and hooks to create lacy, openwork patterns. Accordingly, a gauge range is difficult to determine. Always follow the gauge stated in your pattern.

*** Steel crochet hooks are sized differently from regular hooks--the higher the number, the smaller the hook, which is the reverse of regular hook sizing.

This Standards & Guidelines booklet and downloadable symbol artwork are available at: **YarnStandards.com**

SKILL LEVELS FOR CROCHET

1 ◑☐☐☐ **Beginner** — Projects for first-time crocheters using basic stitches. Minimal shaping.

2 ◑■☐☐ **Easy** — Projects using yarn with basic stitches, repetitive stitch patterns, simple color changes, and simple shaping and finishing.

3 ◑■■☐ **Intermediate** — Projects using a variety of techniques, such as basic lace patterns or color patterns, mid-level shaping and finishing.

4 ◑■■◐ **Experienced** — Projects with intricate stitch patterns, techniques and dimension, such as non-repeating patterns, multicolor techniques, fine threads, small hooks, detailed shaping and refined finishing.

This Standards & Guidelines booklet and downloadable symbol artwork are available at: **YarnStandards.com**

Books

300 Crochet Patterns Book (Japanese). Japan: Nihon Vogue-Sha Co., Ltd., 2006.

Association of Japan Knit Culture. *100 Tunisian Crochet Patterns* (Japanese). Japan: Nihon Vogue-Sha Co. Ltd., 2007.

Barnden, Betty. *The Crochet Stitch Bible.* Iola, WI: Krause Publications, 2004.

Christmas, Carolyn, and Dorris Brooks. *101 Easy Tunisian Stitches.* Berne, IN: Annie's Attic, 2004.

Eckman, Edie. *The Crochet Answer Book.* North Adams, MA: Storey Publishing, 2005.

Haxell, Kate (ed.). *Crochet Edgings & Trims* (The Harmony Guides). Loveland, CO: Interweave Press LLC, 2009.

Knight, Erika (ed.). *Basic Crochet Stitches* (The Harmony Guides). Loveland, CO: Interweave Press LLC, 2008.

Matthews, Anne. *Vogue Dictionary of Crochet Stitches.* Newton, UK: David & Charles, 1987.

Reader's Digest. *The Ultimate Sourcebook of Knitting and Crochet Stitches.* Pleasantville, NY: Reader's Digest, 2003.

Silverman, Sharon Hernes. *Basic Crocheting.* Mechanicsburg, PA: Stackpole Books, 2006.

Silverman, Sharon Hernes. *Beyond Basic Crocheting.* Mechanicsburg, PA: Stackpole Books, 2007.

Silverman, Sharon Hernes. *Tunisian Crochet.* Mechanicsburg, PA: Stackpole Books, 2009.

Silverman, Sharon Hernes. *Crochet Pillows with Traditional and Tunisian Techniques.* Mechanicsburg, PA: Stackpole Books, 2011.

Yarn

Abuelita Yarns
www.abuelitayarns.com
Blue Heron Yarns
www.blueheronyarns.com
Brown Sheep Company, Inc.
www.brownsheep.com
Jojoland
www.jojoland.com
Kangaroo Dyer/Valley Yarns
www.kangaroodyer.com and www.yarn.com
Katia (Fil Katia, S.A.)
www.katia.eu
Lion Brand Yarn Company
www.lionbrand.com
Louet North America
www.louet.com
OnLine (distributed by Knitting Fever)
www.knittingfever.com
Plymouth Yarn Company, Inc.
www.plymouthyarn.com
Sirdar
www.sirdar.co.uk
SpaceCadet Creations
www.spacecadetcreations.com
Textured Yarn Company
www.texturedyarncompany.com

Hooks

ChiaoGoo/Westing Bridge LLC
www.chiaogoo.com
Denise Interchangeable Knitting and Crochet
www.knitdenise.com
Stitch Diva Studios
www.stitchdiva.com

Scarf Pins

Designs by Romi
www.designsbyromi.com

Other Resources for Crocheters

CRAFT YARN COUNCIL OF AMERICA (CYCA)

The craft yarn industry's trade association has educational links and free projects.
www.craftyarncouncil.com

CROCHET GUILD OF AMERICA (CGOA)

The national association for crocheters sponsors conventions, offers classes, and maintains a membership directory.
www.crochet.org

THE NATIONAL NEEDLEARTS ASSOCIATION (TNNA)

This international trade organization represents retailers, manufacturers, distributors, designers, and wholesalers of products for the needlearts market.
www.tnna.org

RAVELRY

This free online community for knitters, crocheters, and other fiber fans is the place to exchange information, get advice, and keep up with everything yarn-related.
www.ravelry.com

Visual Index

Accordion Arrows, 2

Berry Sorbet, 9

Sparkly Scarlet, 14

Crisp Green Apple, 19

Marabou, 24

Changing Tides, 30

Diamond Loop, 35

Champagne Goblets, 40

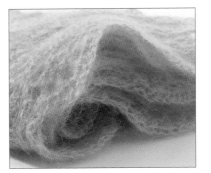

Cactus Lace, 45

Grecian Ladders, 51

Premium Cable, 55

Ambrosia, 63

Classic Plaid, 70

Catch a Weave, 78

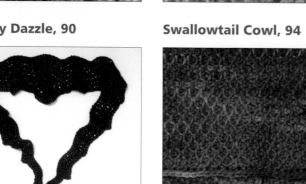

Curly Sunflowers, 86

Holiday Dazzle, 90

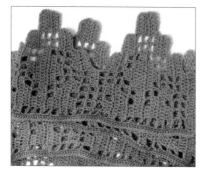

Swallowtail Cowl, 94

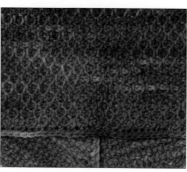

Electric Lime, 99

Monet's Village, 103

Ridged Collar, 107

Sea Splash, 113